PMBOK

Q & A

PROJECT INTEGRATION MANAGEMENT

PROJECT SCOPE MANAGEMENT

PROJECT TIME MANAGEMENT

PROJECT COST MANAGEMENT

PROJECT QUALITY MANAGEMENT

PROJECT HUMAN RESOURCE MANAGEMENT

PROJECT COMMUNICATIONS MANAGEMENT

PROJECT RISK MANAGEMENT

PROJECT PROCUREMENT MANAGEMENT

**A Pocket Guide of Questions & Answers
to Learn More About the
Project Management Body of Knowledge**

PMBOK
Q & A

Project Management Institute
130 South State Rd.
Upper Darby, Pennsylvania 19082 USA
610-734-3330
www.pmi.org

Published by:
Project Management Institute, 130 South State Rd.,
Upper Darby, PA 19082
Phone: 610-734-3330 or Visit our Web Site:
www.pmi.org

ISBN: 1-880410-21-4

Book Team:
James S. Pennypacker, Publisher/Editor-in-Chief
Bobby R. Hensley, Acquisitions Editor
Toni D. Knott, Editor, Book Division
Allison S. Boone, Graphic Designer
Mark S. Parker, Production Coordinator

PMI books are available at special quantity discounts to use as
premiums and sales promotions, or for use in corporate training
programs. For more information, please write to the Business
Manager, PMI Publications Division, 40 Colonial Square, Sylva,
NC 28779. Or Contact your local bookstore.

10   9   8   7   6   5   4   3   2   1

TABLE OF CONTENTS

INTRODUCTION

In the fast-changing and competitive world of project management, more and more project managers are recognizing the importance of developing a deeper understanding of the generally accepted knowledge and practices of the project management profession. The PMBOK Q&A facilitates this goal by offering more than 160 multiple-choice sample questions covering the key themes and concepts of each of the nine areas of *A Guide to the Project Management Body of Knowledge (PMBOK Guide)*, the Project Management Institute's international standard. The answers—regarding integration management, scope management, time management, cost management, quality management, human resource management, communications management, risk management, and procurement management—are provided in the back of the book. The guide's handy pocket size makes it convenient to refer to the book as needed—any time, any where.

Also, as with all publications related to the study of the project management body of knowledge, the PMBOK Q&A may be used to prepare for taking the Project Management Institute's PMP certification examination.

Many people were instrumental in putting together the guide, and, of course, it's impossible to mention all of them. The Project Management Institute would like to thank Lewis Ireland, Walter Taylor, Jim Downer, Terry Borovec, Nancy Krajcar, Marylyn Longo, Sue Spengler, Ahmet Taspinar, Joe Abron, Bob Thompson, Francis Hartman, Dana Littlefield, and David Overbye for their contributions to this valuable project management tool. The questions in this book were an effort of PMI's Service Corps of Project Management Professionals, headed by Ahmet Taspinar. James Henderson with Columbia Assessment Services performed the psychometric review.

PMBOK Q&A
Questions

PROJECT INTEGRATION MANAGEMENT

1. Tools included in Overall Change Control are:

I. Configuration management.
II. Performance measurement.
III. Project management information system.
IV. Performance reports.
V. Project plan updates.

A. I, II, and III only
B. I, III, and IV only
C. II, III, and IV only
D. II, III, and V only
E. III, IV, and V only

2. The Project plan is used to:

A. Finalize budget cost estimates.
B. Facilitate communication among stakeholders.
C. Provide a variable measurement progress.
D. Develop corrective actions.
E. Improve management's general skills.

3. The project performance measurement baselines:

I. Are equivalent to the project plan.
II. Are a management control.
III. Generally change only intermittently.
IV. Document relevant standards.

A. I and III only
B. I and IV only
C. II and III only
D. II and IV only
E. III and IV only

4. Performance measurement baselines should:

A. Remain the same throughout all phases of the project.
B. Change frequently to accommodate current information about the project.
C. Change only intermittently and generally only in response to an approved scope change.
D. Change in order to keep the customer happy.
E. Change only when higher management directs them to be changed.

5. Which process is included in Project Integration Management?

A. Project plan development.
B. Scope planning.
C. Scope definition.
D. Scope verification.
E. Procurement planning.

6. **Identify the Subsidiary Change Control process listed below:**

A. Management systems.
B. Risk change control.
C. Customer interface control systems.
D. Cost estimates.
E. Performance reporting.

7. **Configuration management is any documented procedure used to apply technical administrative direction and surveillance to:**

A. Control cost increases.
B. Identify and correct problems arising in functional areas of project implementation.
C. Identify and document physical characteristics of an item.
D. Test new systems.
E. Estimate and control risk.

8. A Change Control Board is:

A. A formally constituted group of stakeholders responsible for ensuring that only a minimal amount of changes occur on the project.

B. An informal or formal group of team members responsible for changes to a project.

C. An informal group which has oversight of project implementation.

D. A formally constituted group of stakeholders responsible for approving or rejecting changes to the project baselines.

E. The project manager and several key team members working to ensure cost and schedule control during the life of the project.

9. The five basic groups are:

A. Planning, checking, directing, monitoring, and recording.

B. Initiating, planning, executing, controlling, and closing.

C. Planning, executing, monitoring, redirecting, and closing.

D. Planning, executing, directing, closing, and delivering.

E. Initiating, executing, monitoring, evaluating, and closing.

10. **The subprocesses of a project are defined by PMI as having an input, _____, and an output.**

   A. Resolution and action.
   B. Formatting and creation.
   C. Tools and techniques.
   D. Process integration.
   E. Action and integration.

11. **As a function of Project Time Management, the process of developing a schedule is made up of:**

   A. Activity definition, activity sequencing, activity execution, and activity duration.
   B. Activity definition, activity sequencing, and activity duration.
   C. Activity identification, activity execution, and activity results.
   D. Activity identification, activity sequencing, activity connection, and activity duration.
   E. Activity determination, activity duration, activity implementation, and activity results.

12. A controlling process for a project's schedule typically will focus on activities:

A. Starting earlier than scheduled.
B. Starting later than scheduled.
C. That vary from the plan, whether late or early.
D. That are only on the critical path.
E. That are difficult to carry out.

PROJECT SCOPE MANAGEMENT

13. A scope change is defined as a:

A. Change in technical specifications as defined in the WBS.
B. Change in project authorization.
C. Change in project personnel.
D. Modification to the agreed upon project scope as defined in the WBS.
E. Modification to the budget as agreed upon for the project.

14. The scope management plan includes:

I. How changes will be integrated into the project.
II. An assessment of the stability of the project scope.
III. A clear description of how scope changes will be identified and classified.

A. I only
B. III only
C. I and II only
D. I, II, and III

15. The Scope Change Control System should include:

I. Paperwork.
II. Tracking system.
III. Approval levels.
IV. Evaluation process.

A. II and III only
B. I, II, and III only
C. I, II, and IV only
D. I, III, and IV only
E. II, III, and IV only

16. Benefit measurement methods for selecting a project include:

I. Comparative approaches.
II. Economic models.
III. Linear programming methods.
IV. Integer programming models.

A. I and II only
B. I and IV only
C. II and III only
D. III and IV only
E. I, II, III, and IV

17. **Poor scope definition may cause all of the following EXCEPT:**

   A. Higher project costs.
   B. Rework.
   C. Material failure.
   D. Low morale.
   E. Schedule delays.

18. **Scope change control is the process concerned with:**

   I. Influencing factors which create scope change.
   II. Determining that a scope change has occurred.
   III. Managing actual changes when they occur.

   A. I only
   B. III only
   C. I and II only
   D. II and III only
   E. I, II, and III

19. Scope definition is necessary to:

I. Evaluate the project at its completion.
II. Improve the accuracy of cost, time, and resource estimates.
III. Define a baseline for progress measurement and control.
IV. Facilitate clear responsibility assignments.

A. II only
B. III only
C. I and III only
D. II, III, and IV only
E. I, II, III, and IV

20. A code of accounts:

A. Uniquely identifies each element of the WBS.
B. Includes work packages, used to track phase completion.
C. Is an organizational scheme to keep track of contracts.
D. Charts elements of the WBS against the timeline.

21. Scope verification:

A. Is the formal acceptance of the project scope by the stakeholders.
B. Refers to the final project report describing the project at completion.
C. Is not necessary if the project completes on time and on budget.
D. Occurs only when revisions or change orders are made to the project.
E. Details how the cost estimate matches the element of the projects.

22. The change control process should include all of the following EXCEPT:

A. Scope change control.
B. Resource leveling.
C. Contract administration.
D. Quality control.
E. Risk change control.

23. The scope baseline is the original:

A. Project schedule and budget.
B. Description in the project charter.
C. Plan plus or minus approved changes.
D. Performance measure.
E. Starting point for contract negotiations.

24. The project charter is used for all of the following purposes EXCEPT:

A. To recognize the existence of the project.
B. To refer to the business need.
C. To describe the project.
D. To request bids for different phases of a project.
E. To give the project manager authority to apply resources to a project.

25. A stakeholder is a(n):

A. Project engineer.
B. Vineyard field worker.
C. Individual or agency that controls contingency funds.
D. Individual or organization affected by project activities.
E. Organization's corporate attorney.

26. Scope initiation is the process which formally:

I. Recognizes that a new project exists.
II. Appoints the project manager.
III. Recognizes that an existing project should continue into the next phase.
IV. Establishes and describes the need for a project.

A. I only
B. IV only
C. I and II only
D. I and III only
E. III and IV only

27. The project plan should include all of the following EXCEPT:

A. The project charter.
B. The project management approach.
C. Cost estimates.
D. A detailed change management process.
E. Organizational policy.

28. Scope planning for a project is fully described as:

A. The project specification that includes design principles and project objectives.
B. A three-level project work breakdown structure.
C. A written scope statement that includes project justification, major deliverables, and the project objectives.
D. The project charter.
E. The record showing that all project deliverables are completed satisfactorily.

29. Scope definition is:

A. The responsibility of the client to limit the possibility of change orders.
B. Subdividing the major project deliverables into smaller more manageable components.
C. Determining the responses needed to perform project activities.
D. Analysis of activity sequence, duration, and resource requirements.
E. A written statement identifying the quality standards relevant to the project.

30. Which of the following statements is true of the WBS?

A. The WBS is deliverable-oriented.
B. Each level represents an increasing level of detail.
C. The WBS is an unstructured list of activities in chart form.
D. The WBS is the same as the Organizational Breakdown Structure.
E. The WBS refers to the Bill of Material (BOM).

31. The following is an example of a process constraint:

A. A target completion date.
B. A business risk.
C. The threat of a strike by a subcontractor.
D. Relationship with the seller.
E. The method used to measure project performance.

32. Input(s) to scope definition are:

A. The need for a work-around.
B. The type of contract.
C. The scope statement.
D. Work breakdown structure templates.
E. Decomposition.

33. A program is characterized as a:

A. Grouping of related tasks lasting one year or less.
B. Unique undertaking having a definite time period.
C. A grouping of related projects.
D. A project with a cost over $1 million.
E. Sequence of steps constituting a project.

34. All of the following are characteristics of a "work package" EXCEPT:

A. It is a task at the lowest level of any branch of the WBS.
B. It is a summary task at the top level of the WBS.
C. It consists of manageable units of work that can be planned, budgeted, scheduled, and controlled.
D. It usually contains no more than eighty work hours (effort) to complete.
E. It may be broken into steps as Activity Definition.

35. What is the WBS typically used for?

A. As the basis for organizing and defining the total scope of the project.

B. To define the project schedule.

C. To identify the logical person to be project sponsor.

D. To define the level of reporting the seller provides the buyer.

E. As a record of when work elements are assigned to individuals.

PROJECT TIME MANAGEMENT

36. **The main difference between the two types (Arrow Diagramming Method and Precedence Diagramming Method) of the Critical Path Method of scheduling is the:**

A. Placement of the activity on the logic diagram line.
B. Arrow Diagramming Method is a deterministic method whereas the Precedence Diagramming Method is a probabilistic method.
C. Precedence Diagramming Method is a deterministic method whereas the Arrow Diagramming Method is a probabilistic method.
D. Precedence Diagramming Method is a more accurate method.
E. Arrow Diagramming Method is a more accurate method.

37. **The overall duration of the project schedule is influenced by all of the following EXCEPT:**

A. Using mandatory dependencies as constraints.

B. Using discretionary dependencies as constraints.

C. The availability of the resources which are assigned to perform the work.

D. The capabilities of the resources which are assigned to perform the work.

E. Using the Arrow Diagramming Method instead of the Precedence Diagramming Method of scheduling.

38. **The Program Evaluation and Review Technique method of scheduling differs from the Critical Path Method because the PERT method uses:**

A. Weighted averages of activity durations to calculate project duration.

B. "Dummy" activities to represent logic ties.

C. "Free float" instead of "total float" in the schedule calculations.

D. Bar charts instead of logic diagrams to portray the schedule.

E. Segmented network logic.

39. The "fast-tracking" method of schedule compression involves:

A. The use of industrial engineering techniques to improve productivity, thereby finishing the project earlier than originally planned.

B. Work package execution thereby increasing risk.

C. Going on a "mandatory overtime schedule" in order to complete the project earlier.

D. Calculating the percentage of potential schedule overrun, and reducing each activity's duration by that percentage in order to enable the project to complete on schedule.

E. Assigning "dedicated teams" to the critical path activities.

40. The project schedule is useful in the generation of many important documents during the life span of the project. All of the following documents may be generated by a project schedule EXCEPT:

A. Resource Utilization Histograms.

B. Cash Flow Forecasts.

C. Work Breakdown Structure.

D. Performance Measurement Baseline.

E. Purchase Order Curves.

41. **As of the data date, your project schedule has a BCWS of 100. The BCWP, however, is 110. This tells you that your project is currently 10%:**

A. Behind schedule.
B. Ahead of schedule.
C. Over budget.
D. Under budget.
E. Ahead of schedule and over budget.

42. **In what way does Free Float differ from Total Float?**

A. Free Float is the amount of Total Float that does not affect the end date, whereas Total Float is the accumulated amount of Free Float.
B. There is no difference—the two terms are functionally equivalent.
C. Free Float affects only the early start of any immediately following activities.
D. Free Float is commonly referred to as "slack time," whereas Total Float is commonly referred to as "float time."
E. An activity's Free Float is calculated by subtracting its Total Float from the critical path's Total Float.

43. An example of a "soft logic" dependency, as opposed to a "hard logic dependency," is:

A. Project A, the company's participation in a Pump Industry trade show, depends on the successful completion of Project B, which is building the prototype pump that is going to be displayed.

B. To install the plumbing and electrical work at the same time on a single family dwelling.

C. To schedule all unloading of equipment weighing in excess of fifty tons because the daily rent on the crane with that lifting capability is $10,000.

D. For the shrink-wrapping on the finished box of software to depend on enclosing the manual and software first.

E. To schedule the final testing activity of a computer to start seventy-two hours after the mandatory seventy-two hour "burn-in" period.

44. **One way that the Graphical Evaluation and Review Technique differs from the Program Evaluation and Review Technique is that it:**

A. Allows the relationships in the logic diagram to contain loops.

B. Represents the Project Baseline Chart in a superimposed fashion over both the logic diagram and the Gantt Charts.

C. Uses Object Oriented Programming techniques to allow resource histograms that are attached to the project's Gantt Charts.

D. Represents the duration of the project activities in a probabilistic fashion.

E. Represents the duration of the project activities in a deterministic fashion.

45. Your schedule analysis has shown that your project has a high likelihood of experiencing a schedule overrun. You know this because the BCWP is much:

A. Higher than the ACWP.
B. Lower than the ACWP.
C. Higher than the BCWS.
D. Lower than the BCWS.
E. Higher than the CPI.

46. The schedule should be "re-baselined" when:

A. A sequence of activities has taken longer than originally planned.
B. The scope has been increased by the client, with an associated approval of the increase.
C. The productivity within a certain discipline has been higher than originally planned.
D. A high-duration activity has been accomplished "out-of-sequence."
E. Problem experience dictates, in order to justify changes to the client.

47. The key inputs into activity definition are:

A. Work breakdown structure, project schedule, and network diagram.
B. Project schedule, progress reports, and change requests.
C. Project network diagram, constraints, and durations.
D. Work breakdown structure, scope statement, and historical information that supports the applicable activity.
E. Scope statement, work breakdown structure, and changes required.

48. To decrease the total project duration for the least cost is called:

A. Duration compression.
B. Crashing.
C. PERT.
D. ADM or PDM forward and backward pass to determine the critical path.
E. Fast Tracking.

49. A Gantt chart is useful in determining:

A. The level of effort of a task.
B. When a task starts and stops.
C. How tasks are related to each other.
D. Who is assigned to do a task.
E. Relative priority of tasks.

50. A network analysis technique that allows for conditional and probabilistic treatment of logical relationships is known as:

A. The work breakdown structure.
B. The Gantt chart.
C. Time scaled network diagramming.
D. Graphical Evaluation and Review Technique.
E. The Critical Path Method.

51. The Program Evaluation and Review Technique is used for:

A. Developing the work breakdown structure.

B. Developing cost histograms.

C. Estimating project duration when there is a high degree of uncertainty with the individual activity duration estimates.

D. Presenting project summary status to upper management.

E. Determining project duration when it is necessary to factor in the conditional probabilistic treatment of logical relationships.

52. The Precedence Diagramming Method provides project managers with knowledge of:

A. All levels of the work breakdown structure.

B. Tasks likely to be involved in the project integration and resource allocation functions.

C. A graphical representation of the task interdependencies.

D. What the project completion date is.

E. Project duration analysis of which sequence of activities has the least flexibility.

53. Analogous estimating is also called:

A. Bottom-up estimating.
B. Top-down estimating.
C. Multiple duration estimating.
D. Deductive estimating.
E. Inductions estimating.

54. The critical path is calculated by establishing the following dates:

A. Start to start, start to finish, finish to finish, finish to start.
B. Early start, early finish, late start, late finish.
C. Predecessor to successor, predecessor to predecessor, successor to successor.
D. Primary to secondary, primary to finish, secondary to secondary, finish to finish.
E. Planned start, actual start, planned finish, actual finish.

55. Fast Tracking in time management is:

A. Doing some or all activities in parallel rather than in sequence.
B. Preparing progress reports on a quick turn-around basis.
C. The timely input of data to calculate the critical path.
D. Reducing the time allowed for each project activity.
E. Minimizing float.

PROJECT COST MANAGEMENT

56. Project Cost Management includes all of the following functions EXCEPT:

A. Resource planning.
B. Resource leveling.
C. Cost estimating.
D. Cost budgeting.
E. Cost control.

57. Which of the following choices indicates that your project was 10% under budget?

A. The BCWS was 100, and the BCWP was 110.
B. The ACWP was 100, and the BCWP was 110.
C. The BCWS was 100, and the ACWP was 110.
D. The ACWP was 110, and the BCWP was 100.
E. The BCWP was 100, and the BCWS was 110.

58. Earned Value can best be defined as:

A. The value of the equipment that has been installed as of the data date.
B. The sum of the labor costs, which have been incurred on the project to date.
C. A method of measuring project performance.
D. A method of measuring the amount of money that has been spent to date.
E. The Actual Cost of Work Performed minus the Budgeted Cost of Work Performed.

59. The output from resource planning includes:

A. Job descriptions.
B. Salary schedules.
C. The types of resources required.
D. Analogous estimating.
E. Historical information.

60. Cost estimates may be expressed in:

    I.   Units of currency.
   II. Staff hours.
  III. Staff days.

  A. I only
  B. II only
  C. III only
  D. I and II only
  E. I, II, and III

61. All of the following are functions of cost control EXCEPT:

  A. Informing the appropriate project stakeholders of authorized changes in the cost baseline.
  B. Monitoring cost performance to detect variances from the cost baseline.
  C. Ensuring that all appropriate changes are recorded accurately in the cost baseline.
  D. Allocating the overall estimates to individual work packages in order to establish a cost baseline.
  E. Preventing incorrect, inappropriate, or unauthorized changes from being included in the cost baseline.

62. **During the sixth monthly update on a ten-month, $30,000 project, the analysis shows that the BCWS is $20,000, and the ACWP is $10,000. The BCWP is also determined to be $15,000. What can be ascertained from these figures?**

I.   Less has been accomplished than was planned.
II. Less has been spent than planned.
III. To complete the project on schedule, costs will exceed budget.
IV. The project will probably complete behind schedule, but under budget.

A. II only
B. II and III only
C. III and IV only
D. I, II, and IV only
E. I, II, III, and IV

63. **Cost estimates include all of the following resource categories EXCEPT:**

A. Labor.
B. Materials.
C. Supplies.
D. Inflation allowances.
E. Time allocations.

64. Parametric cost estimating involves:

A. Using the work breakdown structure as the basis for estimating.

B. Defining the parameters of the project life cycle.

C. Calculating individual cost estimates for each work package.

D. Using rates and factors based on historical experience to estimate costs.

E. Using the actual cost of a similar project to estimate total project costs.

65. All of the following choices represent inputs to the resource planning process EXCEPT:

A. The policies of the particular organization (e.g., use of contracting or internal staffing, or lease or purchase major equipment).

B. The Work Breakdown Structure.

C. Descriptions of the available resources.

D. The actual final cost of the last project.

E. The scope statement.

66. Cost control is concerned with:

I. Influencing the factors that create change to the cost baseline.
II. Determining that the coast baseline has changed.
III. Managing cost changes when they occur.

A. I only
B. III only
C. I and III only
D. II and III only
E. I, II, and III only

67. Historical results used in cost estimating may include:

I. Project team knowledge.
II. Project files.
III. Commercial cost estimating databases.
IV. Actual time to complete similar projects.

A. I, II, and III only
B. I, II, and IV only
C. I, III, and IV only
D. II, III, and IV only
E. I, II, III, and IV

68. In the earned value system, cost variance is computed as:

A. BCWP less BCWS.
B. BCWP less ACWP.
C. ACWP less BCWP.
D. ACWP less BCWS.
E. BCWS less BCWP.

69. Earned Value includes:

I.   Percent complete.
II. Actual cost of work performed.
III. Completed work value.
IV. Budgeted cost of work performed.

A. III only
B. I and II only
C. II and III only
D. I, III, and IV only
E. I, II, III, and IV

70. Analogous estimating:

A. Uses bottom-up estimating techniques.
B. Uses the actual costs from a previous, similar project.
C. Is used most frequently in the later stages of a project.
D. Uses project characteristics in a mathematical model.
E. Summarizes estimates for individual work items.

71. Inputs to resource planning include all of the following EXCEPT:

A. The WBS.
B. The scope statement.
C. A resource pool description.
D. Organizational policies.
E. Resource requirements.

72. **Of the following four major processes contained in Project Cost Management, which are concerned with the Cost Baseline?**

    A. Resource Planning and Cost Estimating.
    B. Cost Estimating and Cost Budgeting.
    C. Cost Budgeting and Cost Control.
    D. Resource Planning and Cost Control.
    E. Resource Planning, Cost Estimating, and Cost Control.

73. **In order to determine the project's Estimate At Completion, which of the following information is needed?**

    A. The Budgeted Cost of Work Performed and the Actual Cost of Work Performed.
    B. The Budgeted Cost of Work Performed and the Cost Variance.
    C. The Cost Performance Index and the Cost Variance.
    D. The Actual Cost of Work Performed and the Cost Performance Index.
    E. The actuals to date or Actual Cost of Work Performed and the Estimate To Complete.

74. If BCWS = 100, BCWP = 98, and ACWP = 104, the project is:

A. Ahead of schedule.

B. Headed for a cost overrun.

C. Operating at project cost projections.

D. Likely to come in under budget at completion.

E. Behind schedule.

75. Which is an acceptable cause for "re-baselining" a $10 million project?

A. The monthly Consumer Price Index on some commodities essential to the project has gone up by 1.6 percent, an increase of 46 percent over the 1.1 percent that had been budgeted.

B. The client has authorized a $10,000 addition to the scope of the project.

C. The contractor's company has instituted a Quality Program in which it has pledged to spend one million dollars during the next year.

D. The productivity in the Drafting Department is lower than anticipated, which has resulted in 1,000 additional hours, a 78 percent increase over what was budgeted.

E. The Engineering Department has converted to a new $200,000 CAD system.

Questions 76-77:

Item	BCWS	ACWP	BCWP
1	10,000	11,000	10,000
2	9,000	8,000	7,000
3	8,000	8,000	8,000
4	7,000	7,000	5,000
5	6,000	9,000	6,000

76. Which item is MOST over budget?

A. Item 1
B. Item 2
C. Item 3
D. Item 4
E. Item 5

77. Which item has the LOWEST SPI?

A. Item 1
B. Item 2
C. Item 3
D. Item 4
E. Item 5

PROJECT QUALITY MANAGEMENT

78. Inputs to quality control are all of the following EXCEPT:

A. Work results.
B. Quality management plan.
C. Operational definitions.
D. Checklists.
E. Process adjustments.

79. One of the fundamental tenets of quality management is that quality:

A. Exceeds client expectations.
B. Does not cost.
C. Is planned in, not inspected in.
D. Is assured through careful planning.
E. Requires constant monitoring.

80. Standards for products and services are critical to the process of satisfying:

A. Customer requirements.
B. The scope statement.
C. Upper management.
D. Functional requirements.
E. Specifications.

81. All of the following are primary benefit(s) of meeting quality requirements EXCEPT:

A. Less rework.
B. Higher productivity.
C. Lower costs.
D. Stakeholder satisfaction.
E. Fewer change orders.

82. In the quality management discipline, benefits _____ costs.

A. Equal
B. Outweigh
C. Are less than
D. Cannot be evaluated in relation to
E. Are substantiated by

83. "Design of experiments" is an analytical technique that helps:

A. Determine how various elements of a system interrelate.
B. Anticipate what and where quality problems might occur.
C. Identify which variables have the most influence on the overall outcome.
D. Establish a standard by which to measure performance.
E. Compare actual or planned project practices to those of other projects.

84. **The quality management plan provides input to _____ and addresses quality control, quality assurance, and quality improvement.**

   A. The overall project plan
   B. The WBS
   C. The project scope
   D. External stakeholders
   E. Standards and guidelines

85. **Project quality assurance:**

   A. Includes policing the conformance of the project team to specifications.
   B. Provides the project team and stakeholders with standards, by which the project performance is measured.
   C. Is a managerial process that defines the organization, design, resources, and objectives of quality management.
   D. Provides confidence that the project will satisfy relevant quality standards.
   E. Reduces the probability of project completion on schedule.

86. What does "cost of quality" mean?

A. The sacrifice of unessential project objectives to meet essential quality standards.
B. The life cycle cost of the project.
C. The cost of ensuring conformance to requirements.
D. The cost of meeting project objectives.
E. The budgeted allowance for Quality Management activities.

87. The diagram that ranks defects, in the order of frequency of occurrence, using a Histogram to depict 100 percent of the defects, is called a:

A. Pareto diagram.
B. Bar chart.
C. Network diagram.
D. Critical path.
E. Pie chart.

88. Quality standards and criteria should be defined in the _____ phase.

A. Conceptual
B. Planning
C. Implementation
D. Risk identification
E. Communication planning

89. Major cost categories of quality include all of the following EXCEPT:

A. Appraisal.
B. Prevention.
C. External failure.
D. Measurement and test equipment.
E. Computer operations.

90. Investment in defect prevention and appraisal (product quality improvement) must often be borne by:

A. The performing organization.
B. The project management team.
C. Executive management.
D. The project.
E. Overhead costs.

91. Statistical quality control tools include all of the following EXCEPT:

A. Flowcharting.
B. Pareto diagrams.
C. Control charts.
D. Estimates of control tendency.
E. Trend analysis.

92. **The use of quality management tools is essential to provide the greatest degree of:**

A. Satisfaction.
B. Capability.
C. Improvement.
D. Performance.

93. **Quality _____ is evaluating overall project performance on a regular basis to provide confidence that the project will satisfy the relevant quality standards.**

A. Planning
B. Control
C. Assurance
D. Improvement
E. Benchmarking

Project Human Resources Management

94. **The project manager's leadership style should be matched to the corresponding developmental level of the project team and should move through successive steps in the following order:**

   A. Disciplinary, autocratic, and participative.
   B. Projectized, matrix, and functional.
   C. Team building, team development, and responsibility assignment.
   D. Directing, coaching, supporting, and delegating.
   E. Staff planning, team training, and performance monitoring.

95. In selecting from the pool for team assignments, all of the following characteristics should be evaluated EXCEPT:

A. Availability.
B. Personal interest.
C. Personal characteristics.
D. Political philosophy.
E. Previous experience.

96. Human resource administration is the primary responsibility of the:

A. Project Management Team.
B. Human Resources Department.
C. Executive Manager.
D. Line Managers.
E. Project Manager.

97. **A project coordinator may typically be found in a _____ environment.**

    A. Projectized
    B. Strong matrix
    C. Weak matrix
    D. Balance matrix
    E. Phase I

98. **It is important that the staffing plan address how personnel will be released when no longer needed on the project for all of the following reasons EXCEPT:**

    A. To reduce costs.
    B. To improve morale.
    C. To aid in staffing the next project.
    D. To control material resources needed.
    E. To reduce uncertainty.

99. **Motivation factors can be divided into two classes: satisfiers and dissatisfiers. Examples of satisfiers are:**

A. Vacation time, assignment of a personal staff assistant.
B. Work satisfaction, fringe benefits.
C. Plush office space, performance-based salary raise.
D. A sense of personal achievement, work satisfaction.
E. A bonus for completion on time, major recognition events.

100. **A mandatory prerequisite for team building is:**

A. Commitment from top level management.
B. Collocation of team members.
C. Open discussion of poor individual performance.
D. Funding for staff development activities.
E. Shared work ethics among members of the team.

101. Collocation can mean that:

    I.   All team members are moved to a central physical location for the life of the project.

    II. Most team members are moved to a central physical location for the life of the project.

    III. A "war room" is established where team members can meet periodically.

    A. I only
    B. II only
    C. III only
    D. I and III only
    E. I, II, and III

102. For a large, complex project _____ is best for handling cross-functional project needs.

    A. A strong matrix organization
    B. A project coordinator
    C. A project expediter
    D. A functional organization
    E. Direct executive involvement

103. Project Human Resource Management i divided into:

A. Organizational planning, staff acquisitio and performance appraisal.
B. Leadership, team building, and negotiatic
C. Recruitment, labor relations, and personnel administration.
D. Team building, communication, and labc relations.
E. Organizational planning, staff acquisitio and team development.

104. Aids in staff acquisition include all of th following EXCEPT:

A. Staffing management plan.
B. Procurement.
C. Team directory.
D. Training.
E. Negotiation.

105. All of the following are outputs of Organizational Planning EXCEPT:

A. Project organization chart.
B. Staffing management plan.
C. Project template.
D. Supporting detail.
E. Project interfaces.

106. A key barrier to team development is:

A. A strong matrix management structure.
B. When major problems delay the project completion date or budget targets.
C. When team members are accountable to both functional and project managers.
D. When formal training plans cannot be implemented.
E. When members cannot be collocated.

107. All of the following statements about the level of authority of the project manager are true EXCEPT:

A. It varies considerably from company to company.
B. It is dependent on corporate policies.
C. It is determined by senior management.
D. It is weak in a strong matrix organization.
E. It depends on the project manager's philosophy or style.

108. The project manager has the highest level of direct authority in a _____ environment.

A. Strong matrix
B. Weak matrix
C. Projectized
D. Functional
E. Departmentalized

109. In a typical matrix organization, functional managers are responsible for:

I. General administrative philosophy.
II. Assignment of personnel.
III. Developing standards.
IV. Monitoring performance.

A. I only
B. II and IV only
C. I, III, and IV only
D. II, III, and IV only
E. I, II, III, and IV

PROJECT COMMUNICATIONS MANAGEMENT

110. The major processes of project communications management are:

A. Communications requirements, information distribution, performance reporting, and administrative procedures.

B. Communications planning, information distribution, performance reporting and, administrative closure.

C. Communications planning, response planning, progress reporting, and information distribution.

D. Communications planning, information distribution, schedule reporting, and stakeholder analysis.

E. Communications planning, change reporting, project records, and acceptance.

111. The three major types of communication are:

A. Written, oral, and graphic.
B. Written, oral, and visual.
C. Verbal, written, and electronic.
D. Verbal, formal documentation, and informal documentation.
E. Verbal, project records, and computerized.

112. Communication barriers are a more frequent source of conflict in matrix and projectized environments than functional organizations for all the following reasons EXCEPT:

A. Communication is the prime focus of an expediter type of project manager.
B. Team members are often physically separated in a matrix or project environment.
C. There are increased numbers of levels of authority in a matrix or projectized environment.
D. Team members are often separated in the timing of their contributions to a matrix or project environment.
E. Team members with differing skills and backgrounds can be asked to contribute to project results.

113. A communication plan details all of the following EXCEPT:

A. To whom information will flow, and what methods will be used to distribute various types of information.

B. What information will be gathered, how it will be gathered, and how often it will be gathered.

C. Methods for accessing information between scheduled communications.

D. All memos, correspondence, reports, and documents related to the project from all personnel.

E. Production schedules showing when each type of communication will be produced.

114. The three principal reasons for maintaining good document control are:

A. Timely communication, collection of performance appraisal data, and assuring proper disposal of sensitive documents.

B. Timely communication, maintaining proper approvals, and communication cost control.

C. Effective communication, ability to reconstruct why decisions were made, and historical value.

D. Security, change management, and procedural documentation.

E. Security, maintaining proper approvals, and optimizing paperwork flow.

115. Ways to improve listening ability include all of the following EXCEPT:

A. Focusing on concepts and ideas.

B. Listening to feedback.

C. Providing feedback.

D. Performing other activities while the speaker is talking.

E. Allowing the speaker to complete the entire message.

116. Communication barriers between the sender and receiver can include all of the following EXCEPT:

A. Cultural differences.
B. Differences in motivation.
C. Unclear expectations.
D. Shared assumptions.
E. Environmental circumstances.

117. Statements such as "It's never been done before" or "It will cost a fortune" are examples of:

A. Feedback.
B. Communication blockers.
C. Conflict generators.
D. Forcing.
E. Facilitation.

118. The communication "expediter" of a project team is:

A. The MIS subject matter expert.
B. A project manager.
C. A database manager.
D. A project secretary.
E. The project client.

119. All of the following aid in achieving consensus EXCEPT:

A. Avoiding conflict.
B. Maintaining a focus on the problem, not each other.
C. Avoiding voting, trading, or averaging.
D. Avoiding self-oriented behavior.
E. Seeking facts.

120. Inputs to communication planning include:

A. Communications requirements,
communication technology, constraints,
and assumptions.
B. Stakeholder requirements, project logistics,
and project schedule.
C. Stakeholder analysis, communication
barriers, and organizational structure.
D. Communication requirements, project
organization chart, and communication
technology.
E. Stakeholder survey, RAM, WBS, and
administrative procedures.

**121. All of the following are communication
tools EXCEPT:**

A. Memos.
B. Videos.
C. Body Language.
D. Inputting data into a spreadsheet.
E. Verbal circulation of a rumor.

122. **Manual filing systems, electronic text databases, and project management software are examples of:**

A. Information distribution systems.
B. Communications technology.
C. Internal communication systems.
D. Information retrieval systems.
E. Project records.

123. **Most project managers spend about _____ of their work time engaged in some form of communications.**

A. 10 percent
B. 30 percent
C. 50 percent
D. 70 percent
E. 90 percent

124. **All of the following are important if the project manager is to effectively manage communications within the project team EXCEPT:**

A. Formalizing and controlling communication between team members.
B. Promoting harmony and trust between team members.
C. Ensuring that feedback occurs in both directions.
D. Recognizing the importance of the interpersonal communication network.
E. Understanding that communication involves both sending and receiving messages.

125. A "tight matrix" is an organizational option:

A. In which all team members are brought together in one location.
B. Between a weak matrix and a strong matrix.
C. In which functional managers operate in a dual reporting structure reporting to both their own departments and to the project manager.
D. In which project participants act as a coordinated team.
E. In which a functional level of management exists.

126. Communication is the PRIME responsibility of a Project:

A. Expediter.
B. Coordinator.
C. Manager in a weak matrix environment.
D. Manager in a strong matrix environment.
E. Manager in a projectized environment.

127. Communications technology factors include all of the following EXCEPT:

A. Expected staffing levels.
B. Project length.
C. Executive requirements.
D. Availability of technology.
E. Immediacy of the need for information.

128. The best overall effective method of resolving conflict in a project environment is:

A. Smoothing.
B. Withdrawal.
C. Problem solving.
D. Compromise.
E. Confrontation.

129. Tools and techniques for performance reporting include all of the following EXCEPT:

A. Trend analysis.
B. Decision tree analysis.
C. Earned value analysis.
D. Performance reviews.
E. Information distribution tools and techniques.

130. The sender is responsible for:

A. Scheduling communication exchange.
B. Ensuring the receiver agrees with the message.
C. Confirming message is understood.
D. Presenting the message in the most favorable manner.
E. Interpreting the message correctly.

131. Information required to determine project communications requirements typically includes all of the following EXCEPT:

A. Project organization and stakeholder responsibility relationships.
B. Logistics of how many individuals will be involved with the project and at which locations.
C. External information needs, disciplines, departments, and specialties involved in the project.
D. The availability of technology in place at the project location.
E. Project organization and stakeholder responsibility relationship.

132. Formal acceptance by the client or sponsor of the product of the project should be prepared and distributed

_____

A. As part of Administrative Closure.
B. Following the plan as outlined in Quality Management.
C. As requested by upper management.
D. As part of contract close-out.
E. As the last step in project management.

PROJECT RISK MANAGEMENT

133. The categories of risk response development include:

I. Interpretation.
II. Acceptance.
III. Mitigation.
IV. Avoidance.

A. II and III
B. I, II, and III only
C. I, II, and IV only
D. I, III, and IV only
E. II, III, and IV only

134. Risk mitigation could involve:

A. Buying insurance.
B. Policies and procedures for a response system.
C. Accepting a lower profit if some activities overrun.
D. Licensing and intellectual property rights.
E. Eliminating risk through beta testing.

135. Risk identification should be done:

A. Just before a meeting with a client.
B. On a regular basis throughout the project.
C. As soon as time and cost estimates are ready.
D. Early in the execution phase.
E. When preparing the project plan.

136. What is "risk event probability?"

A. An estimate of the probability that an uncontrollable event will occur.
B. The value used in mitigation and deflection.
C. An estimate of the risk value at loss.
D. The probability of the risk not occurring at this time.
E. An estimate of the probability that a given risk will occur.

137. The major processes of project risk management are:

A. Plan, identify, document, and assess.
B. Identify, mitigate, and plan.
C. Respond, evaluate, and document.
D. Identify, quantify, develop, and control.
E. Identify, respond, assess, and document.

138. Outputs from response development could include all of the following EXCEPT:

A. Corrective actions.
B. Risk management plan.
C. Insurance policies.
D. Management reserves.
E. Contingency plans.

139. The tools and techniques for risk quantification are:

A. Contracting, contingency planning, alternate strategies, and insurance.
B. Work-arounds and additional response development.
C. Checklists, damage control reports, standard allowances, and inspection.
D. Checklists, historical results, and interviewing.
E. Expected monetary value, statistical sums, schedule simulations, and decision trees.

140. Response development is sometimes called risk:

A. Identification.
B. Mitigation.
C. Control.
D. Quantification.
E. Action analysis.

141. 1996 PMBOK GUIDE Stakeholder risk tolerances:

A. Provide a mathematical technique that can be used to create a false impression of precision and reliability.

B. Provide a screen or filter to help determine staffing levels.

C. Provide a screen or filter to help determine which project risks to quantify.

D. Is important because different organizations and different individuals have the same tolerances for risk.

E. Are the same for all stakeholders.

142. The outputs from risk quantification include:

A. Opportunities to pursue, threats to respond to.

B. Threats to ignore, opportunities to accept.

C. Threats to respond to, threats to accept.

D. Checklists, corrective actions, and decision trees.

E. Direction, resources, and costs.

143. Acceptance means to:

A. Agree with the project manager.
B. Ignore the consequences.
C. Eliminate a specific threat.
D. Accept the consequences.
E. Purchase insurance.

144. One of the outputs of risk identification is:

A. Potential risk events.
B. Expected monetary value of the risk events.
C. Alternate strategies.
D. Corrective actions.
E. The plan for mitigation.

145. Products or projects that use unproven technologies will, all other things being equal, involve _____ than products or projects using proven technologies.

A. More risk
B. The same risk
C. Less risk
D. Half the risk
E. Twice the risk

146. **A thorough review of _____ will help identify potential opportunities and threats to the project.**

A. Historical results of similar projects
B. The project's change control system
C. The project's mission statement
D. The project's budget
E. Historical data from the project manager's experience

147. **All of the following are inputs to the risk identification process EXCEPT:**

A. WBS.
B. 1996 PMBOK GUIDE staffing plan.
C. Work-around plan.
D. Procurement plan
E. Cost and duration estimates.

148. A risk event description should include all of the following EXCEPT:

A. Event probability.
B. Event frequency.
C. Expected timing.
D. Anticipated mitigation strategy.
E. Alternative outcomes.

149. Expected monetary value is the mathematical product of the:

A. Risk event probability and the risk event value.
B. Risk event probability and beta.
C. Risk event value and sigma.
D. Risk event probability and the standard deviation.
E. Risk event value and beta.

150. Risk response development will utilize which of the following tools?

A. Contracting.
B. Risk Management Plan.
C. Work-arounds.
D. Contingency plan.
E. Corrective action.

151. A risk management plan should include all of the following EXCEPT:

A. Who is responsible for managing various areas of risks.
B. A Work Breakdown Structure.
C. How reserves will be allocated.
D. Risk identification and risk quantification processes.
E. How contingency plans will be implemented.

152. The risk management plan is a major component of the:

A. Project plan.
B. Communication plan.
C. Procurement plan.
D. Contingency plan.
E. Quality management plan.

PROJECT PROCUREMENT MANAGEMENT

153. **When making the project procurement plan, the project manager should consider all of the following EXCEPT:**

A. Preliminary cost estimates.
B. Market conditions.
C. Project funding availability.
D. Application area extensions.
E. Product descriptions.

154. **Procurement documents should have all of the following attributes EXCEPT:**

A. Facilitating accurate and complete responses.
B. Including a complete statement of work.
C. Describing the desired form of response.
D. Including the list of potential bidders/respondents.

155. A Request for Bid differs from a Request for Proposal in that the:

A. Request for Proposal is used when source selection will be price driven.
B. Request for Proposal is used when the project timeframe is limited.
C. Request for Bid is used when source selection will be price driven.
D. Request for Proposal disregards price considerations.
E. Request for Bid is concerned with price exclusively.

156. Contract administration change requests may include all of the following EXCEPT:

A. Modifications to the terms of the contract.
B. Termination of the contract if the seller's work is unsatisfactory.
C. Modification to the description of the product or service to be provided.
D. Seller invoices.
E. Contracted changes.

157. Which of the following is true about the advertising in the solicitation process?

I. It is sometimes required on public projects.
II. It is an effective method of expanding the list of potential bidders.
III. It can cause public pressure resulting in bid disputes.

A. I only
B. II only
C. I and II only
D. I and III only
E. I, II, and III

158. Which type of contract provides the highest risk to the Owner (Buyer)?

A. Cost Plus Percentage of Cost.
B. Cost Plus Fixed Fee.
C. Firm Fixed Price.
D. Fixed Price Plus Incentive Fee.
E. Cost Plus Incentive Fee.

159. In negotiations, what is a *fait accompli* tactic?

A. Accomplishing the phase before the other side is ready.
B. Pretending to accept the other side's offer.
C. Claiming an issue has already been decided on and cannot be changed.
D. Acting in good faith.
E. Promising that a requirement will be completed before it is due.

160. An expressed warranty:

A. Is provided by the sales manager.
B. Is a statement of the characteristics of the product.
C. Covers a longer period than the implied warranty.
D. Is the best guarantee to the buyer.
E. Can be sold separately.

161. The project's contractor payment system should include:

A. An administrative review.
B. The contractor submission.
C. A review of work performed.
D. Negotiations over price.
E. A viable account payable system.

162. The contract administrator should provide _____ at formal closure of the project.

I. Formal notice of project completion to the contractor
II. Letters of commendation to all project staff
III. Formal notice of acceptance to the contractor
IV. Internal notice to senior management/buyer

A. I only
B. IV only
C. I and III only
D. II and IV only
E. I, III, and IV only

163. Which type of contract should be used for a well-defined product?

A. Unit price contract.
B. Fixed price contract.
C. Cost reimbursable contract.
D. Partnership contract.
E. A unit price contract that disallows such contracting.

164. Contract close-out documentation includes all of the following EXCEPT:

A. Technical documentation.
B. Financial documents.
C. The RFP or RFB and seller's working proposal.
D. Results of contract-related inspections.

165. Potential contract changes should be:

A. Postponed as long as possible to protect the budget.

B. Viewed as negative, quantified, and tabulated.

C. Quantified and fed back through the project planning and procurement processes.

D. Reviewed by senior management and the buyer.

E. Submitted for bids to the relevant vendor list.

166. The purpose of a procurement audit is to do all of the following EXCEPT:

A. Maintain a complete file of contract-related records.

B. Determine if all required work has been completed.

C. Determine if the bid documents used were effective.

D. Determine if the contract change control system was effective.

E. Identify successes and failures and their implications.

167. When the procurement item is available from only one supplier, all of the following evaluation criteria should be identified and documented to support an integrated assessment EXCEPT:

A. Management approach.
B. Financial capacity.
C. Life cycle cost.
D. Technical capabilities.
E. Mode of delivery.

168. All of the following methods are available to the project manager for short-listing contractor proposals EXCEPT:

A. Comparing proposals against independent estimates.
B. Weighting systems.
C. Subjective screening systems.
D. Resource distribution system.
E. Negotiation.

169. Which terms are used to describe contested changes when the seller and project management team disagree on compensation for the change?

I. Appeals.
II. Mediation.
III. Claims.
IV. Disputes.
V. Arbitration.

A. I and III only
B. II and IV only
C. IV and V only
D. I, III, and IV only
E. II, III, and V only

170. FFP is an acronym for:

A. Free Flow Performance.
B. Fundamentally Fixed Price.
C. Firm Fixed Price.
D. Free Form Project.
E. Fixed File Procurement.

PROJECT INTEGRATION
MANAGEMENT ANSWERS

1. Answer: A.
PMBOK GUIDE page 41, Figure 4-1 (4.3), and page 44,
Section 4.3

Tools and Techniques:
.1 Change control system
.2 Configuration management
.3 Performance measurement
.4 Additional planning
.5 Project management information system

2. Answer: B.
PMBOK GUIDE pages 39–40

The project plan is used to:
- Guide project execution.
- Document project planning assumptions.
- Document project planning decisions regarding alternatives chosen.
- Facilitate communication among stakeholders.
- Define key management reviews as to content, extent, and timing.
- Provide a baseline for progress measurement and project control.

3. Answer: C.
PMBOK GUIDE, page 42, 4.1.3.1

The project plan is a document or collection of documents that should be expected to change over time as more information becomes available about the project. The performance measurement baselines represent a *management control* that will generally change only intermittently and then generally only in response to an approved scope change.

4. Answer: C.
PMBOK GUIDE, page 42, 4.1.3.1

The performance measurement baselines represent a management control that will generally change only intermittently and then generally only in response to an approved scope change.

5. Answer: A.
PMBOK GUIDE, page 39

While all project management processes are integrative to some extent, the processes described in this chapter are *primarily* integrative. **Figure 4-1** provides an overview of the following major processes:

4.1 Project Plan Development—taking the results of other planning processes and putting them into a consistent, coherent document.

4.2 Project Plan Execution—carrying out the project plan by performing the activities included therein.

4.3 Overall Change Control—coordinating changes across the entire project.

6. Answer: B.
PMBOK GUIDE page 45, Figure 4-2

Subsidiary Change Control
- Scope Change Control
- Schedule Change Control
- Cost Change Control
- Quality Control
- Risk Change Control
- Contract Administration

7. Answer: C.
PMBOK GUIDE, page 45

Configuration management is any documented procedure used to apply technical and administrative direction and surveillance to:
- Identify and document the functional and physical characteristics of an item or system.
- Control any changes to such characteristics.
- Record and report the change and its implementation status.
- Audit the items and system to verify conformance to requirements[1].

8. Answer: D.

PMBOK GUIDE Glossary, page 160

> **Change Control Board (CCB).** A formally constituted group of stakeholders responsible for approving or rejecting changes to the project *baselines*.

9. Answer: B.

PMBOK GUIDE, page 28

> Project management processes can be organized into five groups of one or more processes each:
> - Initiating processes—recognizing that a project or phase should begin and committing to do so.
> - Planning processes—devising and maintaining a workable scheme to accomplish the business need that the project was undertaken to address.
> - Executing processes—coordinating people and other resources to carry out the plan.
> - Controlling processes—ensuring that project objectives are met by monitoring and measuring progress and taking corrective action when necessary.
> - Closing processes—formalizing acceptance of the project or phase and bringing it to an orderly end.

10. Answer: C.
PMBOK GUIDE, page 29

Within each process group, the individual processes are linked by their inputs and outputs. By focusing on these links, we can describe each process in terms of its:
- Inputs—documents or documentable items that will be acted upon.
- Tools and techniques—mechanisms applied to the inputs to create the outputs.
- Outputs—documents or documentable items that are a result of the process.

11. Answer: B.

PMBOK GUIDE Summary, page 151

A subset of project management that includes the processes required to ensure timely completion of the project. It consists of:

- Activity definition—identifying the specific activities that must be performed to produce the various project deliverables.
- Activity sequencing—identifying and documenting interactivity dependencies.
- Activity duration estimating—estimating the number of work periods which will be needed to complete individual activities.
- Schedule development—analyzing activity sequences, activity durations, and resource requirements to create the project schedule.
- Schedule control—controlling changes to the project schedule.

12. Answer: C.

PMBOK GUIDE, page 32, 3.3.4

Project performance must be measured regularly to identify variances from the plan. Variances are fed into the control processes in the various knowledge areas. To the extent that significant variances are observed (i.e., those that jeopardize the project objectives), adjustments to the plan are made by repeating the appropriate project planning processes. For example, a missed activity finish date may require adjustments to the current staffing plan, reliance on overtime, or trade-offs between budget and schedule objectives. Controlling also includes taking preventive action in anticipation of possible problems.

PROJECT SCOPE MANAGEMENT ANSWERS

13. ANSWER: D.
PMBOK GUIDE page 58, 5.5.3.1

A scope change is any modification to the agreed-upon project scope as defined by the approved WBS.

14. ANSWER: D.
PMBOK GUIDE page 52, 5.2.3.3

Scope management plan. This document describes how project scope will be managed and how scope changes will be integrated into the project. It should also include an assessment of the expected stability of the project scope (i.e., how likely is it to change, how frequently, and by how much). The scope management plan should also include a clear description of how scope changes will be identified and classified (this is particularly difficult—and therefore absolutely essential—when the product characteristics are still being elaborated).

15. ANSWER: B.
PMBOK GUIDE page 58, 5.5.2.1

A scope change control system defines the procedures by which the project scope may be changed. It includes the paperwork, tracking systems, and approval levels necessary for authorizing changes. The scope change control system should be integrated with the overall change control system. . . .

16. ANSWER: E.
PMBOK GUIDE page 50, 5.1.2.1

Project selection methods. Project selection methods generally fall into one of two broad categories [2]:
- Benefit measurement methods—comparative approaches, scoring models, benefit contribution, or economic models.
- Constrained optimization methods—mathematical models using linear, dynamic, integer, and multi-objective programming algorithms.

17. ANSWER: C.

PMBOK GUIDE page 52, 5.3

Proper scope definition is critical to project success. "When there is poor scope definition, final project costs can be expected to be higher because of the inevitable changes which disrupt project rhythm, cause rework, increase project time, and lower the productivity and morale of the workforce" [3].

18. ANSWER: E.

PMBOK GUIDE page 57, 5.5

Scope change control is concerned with (a) influencing the factors which create scope changes to ensure that changes are beneficial, (b) determining that a scope change has occurred, and (c) managing the actual changes when and if they occur.

19. ANSWER: D.
PMBOK GUIDE page 52, 5.3

Scope definition involves subdividing the major project deliverables (as identified in the scope statement) into smaller, more manageable components in order to:
- Improve the accuracy of cost, time, and resource estimates.
- Define a baseline for performance measurement and control.
- Facilitate clear responsibility assignments.

20. ANSWER: A.
PMBOK GUIDE Glossary, pages 160 and 171

Code of Accounts. Any numbering system used to uniquely identify each element of the *work breakdown structure*.
Work Package. A deliverable at the lowest level of the *work breakdown structure*.

21. ANSWER: A.
PMBOK GUIDE page 56, 5.4

Scope verification is the process of formalizing acceptance of the project scope by the stakeholders (sponsor, client, customer, etc.).

22. ANSWER: B.
PMBOK GUIDE page 45, Figure 4-2

Subsidiary Change Control
- Scope Change Control
- Schedule Change Control
- Cost Change Control
- Quality Control
- Risk Change Control
- Contract Administration

23. ANSWER: C.
PMBOK GUIDE Glossary, page 160

Baseline. The original plan (for a project, a work package, or an activity), plus or minus approved changes. Usually used with a modifier (e.g., cost baseline, schedule baseline, performance measurement baseline).

24. ANSWER: D.
PMBOK GUIDE page 50, 5.1.3.1

A project charter is a document that formally
recognizes the existence of a project. It should
include, either directly or by reference to other
documents:
* The business need that the project was
  undertaken to address.
* The product description. . . .

25. ANSWER: D.
PMBOK GUIDE Glossary, page 170

Stakeholder. Individuals and organizations
who are involved in or may be affected by
project activities.

26. ANSWER: D.
PMBOK GUIDE page 49, 5.1

Initiation is the process of formally recognizing
that a new project exists or that an existing
project should continue into its next phase. . . .

27. ANSWER: E.
PMBOK GUIDE page 42, 4.1.3.1

There are many ways to organize and present the project plan, but it commonly includes all of the following (these items are described in more detail elsewhere):

- Project charter.
- A description of the project management approach or strategy (a summary of the individual management plans from the other knowledge areas).
- Scope statement, which includes the project deliverables and the project objectives.
- Work breakdown structure (WBS) to the level at which control will be exercised.
- Cost estimates, scheduled start dates, and responsibility assignments to the level of the WBS at which control will be exercised.
- Performance measurement baselines for schedule and cost.
- Major milestones and target dates for each.
- Key or required staff.
- Key risks, including constraints and assumptions, and planned responses for each.
- Subsidiary management plans, including scope management plan, schedule management plan, etc.
- Open issues and pending decisions.

28. ANSWER: C.
PMBOK GUIDE Glossary, page 170

Scope Planning. Developing a written scope statement that includes the project justification, the major deliverables, and the project objectives.

29. ANSWER: B.
PMBOK GUIDE Glossary, page 170

Scope Definition. Decomposing the major deliverables into smaller, more manageable components to provide better control.

30. ANSWER: A.
PMBOK GUIDE page 54, 5.3.3.1

A work breakdown structure is a deliverable-oriented grouping of project elements that organizes and defines the total scope of the project: work not in the WBS is outside the scope of the project.

31. ANSWER: A.
PMBOK GUIDE page 35, 3.4, and page 50, 5.1.3.3

Some process outputs may be predefined as constraints. For example, management may specify a target completion date rather than allowing it to be determined by the planning process (35).

Constraints are factors that will limit the project management team's options. For example, a predefined budget is a constraint that is highly likely to limit the team's options regarding scope, staffing, and schedule (50).

32. ANSWER: C.
PMBOK GUIDE page 53, 5.3.1, chart

Inputs [to scope definition]
.1 Scope statement
.2 Constraints
.3 Assumptions
.4 Other planning outputs
.5 Historical information

33. ANSWER: C.
PMBOK GUIDE Glossary, page 167

> **Program.** A group of related projects managed in a coordinated way.

34. ANSWER: B.
PMBOK GUIDE Glossary, page 171

> **Work Package.** A deliverable at the lowest level of the *work breakdown structure*. A work package may be divided into activities.

35. ANSWER: A.
PMBOK GUIDE page 54, 5.3.3.1

> A work breakdown structure is a deliverable-oriented grouping of project elements that organizes and defines the total scope of the project: work not in the WBS is outside the scope of the project.

PROJECT TIME MANAGEMENT ANSWERS

36. ANSWER: A.
PMBOK GUIDE, page 63, 6.2.2.1

Precedence diagramming method (PDM). This is a method of constructing a project network diagram using nodes to represent the activities and connecting them with arrows that show the dependencies. . . . This technique is also called *activity-on-node* (AON) and is the method used by most project management software packages.

Arrow diagramming method (ADM). This is a method of constructing a project network diagram using arrows to represent the activities and connecting them at nodes to show the dependencies. . . . This technique is also called *activity-on arrow* (AOA) and, although less prevalent than PDM, is still the technique of choice in some application areas.

37. ANSWER: E.

PMBOK GUIDE, page 62, 6.2.1.3 and 6.2.1.4, and page 65, 6.3.1.4 and 6.3.1.5

Mandatory dependencies are those which are inherent in the nature of the work being done (62, 6.2.1.3).

Discretionary dependencies are those which are defined by the project management team. They should be used with care (and fully documented) since they may limit later scheduling options (62, 6.2.1.4).

Resource requirements. . . . The duration of most activities will be significantly influenced by the resources assigned to them (65, 6.3.1.4).

Resource capabilities. The duration of most activities will be significantly influenced by the capabilities of the humans and material resources assigned to them (65, 6.3.1.5).

38. ANSWER: A.
PMBOK GUIDE, page 67, 6.4.2.1

- Critical Path Method (CPM)—calculates a single, deterministic early and late start and finish date for each activity based on specified, sequential network logic and a single duration estimate.
- Program Evaluation and Review Technique (PERT)—uses sequential network logic and a weighted average duration estimate to calculate project duration. Although there are surface differences, PERT differs from CPM primarily in that it uses the distribution's mean (expected value) instead of the most likely estimate originally used in CPM. . . .

39. ANSWER: B.
PMBOK GUIDE page 68, 6.4.2.2

- Fast tracking—doing activities in parallel that would normally be done in sequence. . . . Fast tracking often results in rework and usually increases risk.

40. ANSWER: C.
PMBOK GUIDE page 61, 6.1.1.1

6.1.1 Inputs to Activity Definition
.1 Work breakdown structure. The work breakdown structure is the primary input to activity definition. . . .

41. ANSWER: B.
PMBOK GUIDE Glossary, page 160

Budgeted Cost of Work Performed (BCWP). The sum of the approved costs estimates (including any overhead allocation) for activities (or portions of activities) completed during a given period (usually project-to-date).
Budgeted Cost of Work Scheduled (BCWS). The sum of the approved cost estimates (including any overhead allocation) for activities (or portions of activities) scheduled to be performed during a given period (usually project-to-date).

42. ANSWER: C.
PMBOK GUIDE Glossary, page 164

> **Float.** The amount of time that an activity may be delayed from its early start without delaying the project finish date.
>
> **Free Float (FF).** The amount of time an activity can be delayed without delaying the early start of any immediately following activities.

43. ANSWER: B.
PMBOK GUIDE, pages 62–63, 6.2.1.3–6.2.1.4

- Mandatory dependencies are those which are inherent in the nature of the work being done. They often involve physical limitations (on a construction project it is impossible to erect the superstructure until after the foundation has been built; on an electronics product, a prototype must be built before it can be tested). Mandatory dependencies are also called *hard logic*.
- Discretionary dependencies are those which are defined by the project management team. They should be used with care (and fully documented) since they may limit later scheduling options. . . . Discretionary dependencies may also be called *preferred logic*, *preferential logic*, or *soft logic*.

44. ANSWER: A.
PMBOK GUIDE page 63, 6.2.2.3, and page 67, 6.4.2.1

Diagramming techniques such as GERT (Graphical Evaluation and Review Technique) and System Dynamics models allow for non-sequential activities such as loops (e.g., a test that must be repeated more than once) or conditional branches (e.g., a design update that is only needed if the inspection detects errors). Neither PDM nor ADM allow loops or conditional branches (63, 6.2.2.3).

Program Evaluation and Review Technique (PERT)—uses sequential network logic and a weighted average duration estimate to calculate project duration (67, 6.4.2.1).

45. ANSWER: D.
PMBOK GUIDE page 108, 10.3.2.4

Earned value analysis in its various forms is the most commonly used method of performance measurement. It integrates scope, cost, and schedule measures to help the project management team assess project performance. Earned value involves calculating three key values for each activity:

- The budget, also call the budgeted cost of work scheduled (BCWS), is that portion of the approved cost estimate planned to be spent on the activity during a given period.
- The actual cost, also called the actual cost of work performed (ACWP), is the total of direct and indirect costs incurred in accomplishing work on the activity during a given period.
- The earned value, also called the budgeted cost of work performed (BCWP), is a percentage of the total budget equal to the percentage of the work actually completed. . . .

These three values are used in combination to provide measures of whether or not work is being accomplished as planned. The most commonly used measures are the cost variance (CV = BCWP – ACWP), the schedule variance (SV = BCWP – BCWS), and the cost performance index (CPI = BCWP/ACWP).

46. ANSWER: B.
PMBOK GUIDE Glossary, page 160

> **Baseline.** The original plan (for a project, a work package, or an activity), plus or minus approved changes. Usually used with a modifier (e.g., cost baseline, schedule baseline, performance measurement baseline).

47. ANSWER: D.
PMBOK GUIDE page 60, Figure 6-1, and page 61, 6.1.1

6.1.1 Inputs to Activity Definition
.1 *Work breakdown structure.*
.2 *Scope statement.*
.3 *Historical information.*
.4 *Constraints*
.5 *Assumptions.*

48. ANSWER: B.
PMBOK GUIDE page 68, 6.4.2.2, and Glossary, page 162

Crashing—in which cost and schedule trade-offs are analyzed to determine how to obtain the greatest amount of compression for the least incremental cost (68).

Crashing. Taking action to decrease the total project duration after analyzing a number of alternatives to determine how to get the maximum duration compression for the least cost (162).

49. ANSWER: B.
PMBOK GUIDE page 70, 6.4.3

Bar charts, also called Gantt charts . . . show activity start and end dates as well as expected durations, but do not usually show dependencies. They are relatively easy to read and are frequently used in management presentations.

50. ANSWER: D.
PMBOK GUIDE page 67, 6.4.2.1

Graphical Evaluation and Review Technique (GERT)—allows for probabilistic treatment of both network logic and activity duration estimates. . . .

51. ANSWER: C.
PMBOK GUIDE Glossary, page 167

Program Evaluation and Review Technique (PERT). An event-oriented network analysis technique used to estimate project duration when there is a high degree of uncertainty with the individual activity duration estimates.

52. ANSWER: C.
PMBOK GUIDE page 63, 6.2.2.1 and Figure 6-2

Precedence diagramming method (PDM). This is a method of constructing a project network diagram using nodes to represent the activities and connecting them with arrows that show the dependencies. . . .

53. **ANSWER: B.**
PMBOK GUIDE page 66, 6.3.2.2

Analogous estimating, also called *top-down estimating,* means using the actual duration of a previous, similar activity as the basis for estimating the duration of a future activity.

54. **ANSWER: B.**
PMBOK GUIDE page 67, 6.4.2.1

Critical Path Method (CPM)—calculates a single, deterministic early and late start and finish date for each activity based on specified, sequential network logic and a single duration estimate.

55. **ANSWER: A.**
PMBOK GUIDE page 68, 6.4.2.2

Fast tracking—doing activities in parallel that would normally be done in sequence (e.g., starting to write code on a software project before the design is complete, or starting to build the foundation for a petroleum processing plant before the 25 percent of engineering point is reached). Fast tracking often results in rework and usually increases risk.

PROJECT COST MANAGEMENT ANSWERS

56. ANSWER: B.
PMBOK GUIDE, page 73

Project Cost Management includes the processes required to ensure that the project is completed within the approved budget. . . .

7.1 Resource Planning—determining what resources (people, equipment, materials) and what quantities of each should be used to perform project activities.

7.2 Cost Estimating—developing an approximation (estimate) of the costs of the resources needed to complete project activities.

7.3 Cost Budgeting—allocating the overall cost estimate to individual work items.

7.4 Cost Control—controlling changes to the project budget.

57. ANSWER: B.
PMBOK GUIDE page 108, 10.3.2.4

The most commonly used measures are the cost variance (CV = BCWP [budgeted cost of work performed] – ACWP [actual cost of work performed]). . . .

58. ANSWER: C.
PMBOK GUIDE page 108, 10.3.2.4

Earned value analysis in its various forms is the most commonly used method of performance measurement. It integrates scope, cost, and schedule measures to help the project management team assess project performance.

59. ANSWER: C.
PMBOK GUIDE page 76, 7.1.3

The output of the resource planning process is a description of what types of resources are required and in what quantities for each element of the work breakdown structure.

60. ANSWER: E
PMBOK GUIDE page 78, 7.2.3.1

Cost estimates are generally expressed in units of currency (dollars, francs, yen, etc.) in order to facilitate comparisons both within and across projects. Other units such as staff hours or staff days may be used, unless doing so will misstate project costs (e.g., by failing to differentiate among resources with very different costs).

61. ANSWER: D.
PMBOK GUIDE page 79, 7.4

Cost control includes:
- Monitoring cost performance to detect variances from plan.
- Ensuring that all appropriate changes are recorded accurately in the cost baseline.
- Preventing incorrect, inappropriate, or unauthorized changes from being included in the cost baseline.
- Informing appropriate stakeholders of authorized changes.

62. ANSWER: D.

PMBOK GUIDE page 108, 10.3.2.4

These three values are used in combination to provide measures of whether or not work is being accomplished as planned. The most commonly used measures are the cost variance (CV = BCWP–ACWP), the schedule variance (SV = BCWP–BCWS), and the cost performance index (CPI = BCWP/ACWP). The cumulative CPI (the sum of all individual BCWPs divided by the sum of all individual ACWPs) is widely used to forecast project cost at completion. In some application areas, the schedule performance index (SPI = BCWP/BCWS) is used to forecast the project completion date.

63. ANSWER: E.

PMBOK GUIDE page 78, 7.2.3.1

Cost estimates must be estimated for all resources that will be charged to the project. This includes, but is not limited to, labor, materials, supplies, and special categories such as an inflation allowance or cost reserve.

64. ANSWER: D.
PMBOK GUIDE page 77, 7.2.2.2

Both the cost and accuracy of parametric models varies widely. They are most likely to be reliable when (a) the historical information used to develop the model was accurate, (b) the parameters used in the model are readily quantifiable, and (c) the model is scalable (i.e., it works as well for a very large project as for a very small one).

65. ANSWER: D.
PMBOK GUIDE, page 74, Figure 7-1, and page 75, 7.1.1

7.1.1 Inputs to Resource Planning
.1 Work breakdown structure.
.2 Historical information.
.3 Scope statement.
.4 Resource pool description.
.5 Organizational policies.

66. ANSWER: E.
PMBOK GUIDE page 79, 7.4

> Cost control is concerned with (a) influencing
> the factors which create changes to the cost
> baseline to ensure that changes are beneficial,
> (b) determining that the cost baseline has
> changed, and (c) managing the actual changes
> when and as they occur.

67. ANSWER: A.
PMBOK GUIDE page 77, 7.2.1.5

> *Historical information.* Information on the
> cost of many categories of resources is often
> available from one or more of the following
> sources:
> - Project files. . . .
> - Commercial cost estimating databases. . . .
> - Project team knowledge. . . .

68. ANSWER: B.
PMBOK GUIDE page 108, 10.3.2.4

These three values are used in combination to provide measures of whether or not work is being accomplished as planned. The most commonly used measures are the cost variance (CV = BCWP – ACWP). . . .

69. ANSWER: D.
PMBOK GUIDE page 108, 10.3.2.4

The earned value, also called the budgeted cost of work performed (BCWP), is a percentage of the total budget equal to the percentage of the work actually completed.

70. ANSWER: B.
PMBOK GUIDE page 77, 7.2.2.1

Analogous estimating, also called *top-down estimating,* means using the actual cost of a previous, similar project as the basis for estimating the cost of the current project.

71. ANSWER: E.
PMBOK GUIDE page 75, 7.1.1

> ### 7.1.1 Inputs to Resource Planning
> .1 *Work breakdown structure.*
> .2 *Historical information.*
> .3 *Scope statement.*
> .4 *Resource pool description.*
> .5 *Organizational policies.*

72. ANSWER: C.
PMBOK GUIDE pages 79–80

> ### 7.3.3 Outputs from Cost Budgeting
> .1 *Cost baseline* (79).
>
> ### 7.4.1 Inputs to Cost Control
> .1 *Cost baseline* (80).

73. ANSWER: E.
PMBOK GUIDE page 81, 7.4.3.4

An estimate at completion (EAC) is a forecast of total project costs based on project performance. The most common forecasting techniques are some variation of:

- EAC = Actuals to date plus the remaining project budget modified by a performance factor, often the cost performance index. . . .
- EAC = Actuals to date plus a new estimate for all remaining work. . . .
- EAC = Actuals to date plus remaining budget.

74. ANSWER: B.
PMBOK GUIDE page 108, 10.3.2.4

These three values are used in combination to provide measures of whether or not work is being accomplished as planned. The most commonly used measures are the cost variance (CV = BCWP – ACWP), the schedule variance (SV = BCWP – BCWS), and the cost performance index (CPI = BCWP/ACWP). The cumulative CPI (the sum of all individual BCWPs divided by the sum of all individual ACWPs) is widely used to forecast project cost at completion. In some application areas, the schedule performance index (SPI = BCWP/BCWS) is used to forecast the project completion date.

75. ANSWER: B.
PMBOK GUIDE Glossary, page 160

> **Baseline.** The original plan (for a project, a work package, or an activity), plus or minus approved changes. Usually used with a modifier (e.g., cost baseline, schedule baseline, performance measurement baseline).

76. ANSWER: E.
PMBOK GUIDE page 108, 10.3.2.4

> The most commonly used measures are the cost variance (CV = BCWP − ACWP), the schedule variance (SV = BCWP − BCWS), and the cost performance index (CPI = BCWP/ACWP). The cumulative CPI (the sum of all individual BCWPs divided by the sum of all individual ACWPs) is widely used to forecast project cost at completion. In some application areas, the schedule performance index (SPI = BCWP/BCWS) is used to forecast the project completion date.

77. ANSWER: D.
PMBOK GUIDE page 108, 10.3.2.4

> See #76.

PROJECT QUALITY MANAGEMENT ANSWERS

78. ANSWER: E.
PMBOK GUIDE page 89, 8.3.1

8.3.1 Inputs to Quality Control
.1 *Work results.*
.2 *Quality management plan.*
.3 *Operational definitions.*
.4 *Checklists.*

79. ANSWER: C.
PMBOK GUIDE page 85, 8.1

The project team should also be aware of one
of the fundamental tenets of modern quality
management—quality is planned in, not
inspected in.

80. ANSWER: A.
PMBOK GUIDE page 84

The project management team should also be aware that modern quality management complements modern project management. For example, both disciplines recognize the importance of:

• Customer satisfaction—understanding, managing, and influencing needs so that customer expectations are met or exceeded.

81. ANSWER: E.
PMBOK GUIDE page 86, 8.1.2.1

The primary benefit of meeting quality requirements is less rework, which means higher productivity, lower costs, and increased stakeholder satisfaction.

82. ANSWER: B.
PMBOK GUIDE page 86, 8.1.2.1

It is axiomatic of the quality management discipline that the benefits outweigh the costs.

83. ANSWER: C.
PMBOK GUIDE page 87, 8.1.2.4

Design of experiments is an analytical technique which helps identify which variables have the most influence on the overall outcome.

84. ANSWER: A.
PMBOK GUIDE page 87, 8.1.3.1

The quality management plan provides input to the overall project plan. . . .

85. ANSWER: D.
PMBOK GUIDE page 88, 8.2

Quality assurance is all the planned and systematic activities implemented within the quality system to provide confidence that the project will satisfy the relevant quality standards [6].

86. ANSWER: C.
PMBOK GUIDE Glossary, page 161

> **Cost of Quality.** The costs incurred to ensure quality. The cost of quality includes quality planning, quality control, quality assurance, and rework.

87. ANSWER: A.
PMBOK GUIDE page 90, 8.3.2.3

> A Pareto diagram is a histogram, ordered by frequency of occurrence, that shows how many results were generated by type or category of identified cause. . . .

88. ANSWER: B.
PMBOK GUIDE page 31, Figure 3-5,
and page 32, 3.3.2

> Although these *facilitating processes* are performed intermittently and as needed during project planning, they are not optional. They include:
> • Quality Planning (8.1)—identifying which quality standards are relevant to the project and determining how to satisfy them.

89. ANSWER: E.

PMBOK GUIDE page 89, 8.3, and
page 90, 8.3.2

The project management team should have a
working knowledge of statistical quality
control, especially sampling and probability, to
help them evaluate quality control outputs.
Among other subjects, they should know the
differences between:

- Prevention (keeping errors out of the
  process) and inspection (keeping errors out
  of the hands of the customer).
- Attribute sampling (the result conforms or it
  does not) and variables sampling (the result
  is rated on a continuous scale that measures
  the degree of conformity).
- Special causes (unusual events) and random
  causes (normal process variation).
- Tolerances (the result is acceptable if it falls
  within the range specified by the tolerance)
  and control limits (the process is in control if
  the result falls within the control limits)(89).

8.3.2 Tools and Techniques for Quality Control

.1 Inspection. Inspection includes activities
such as measuring, examining, and testing
undertaken to determine whether results
conform to requirements (90).

90. ANSWER: A.
PMBOK GUIDE page 85, paragraph 2

> However, there is an important difference that the project management team must be acutely aware of—the temporary nature of the project means that investments in product quality improvement, especially defect prevention and appraisal, must often be borne by the performing organization since the project may not last long enough to reap the rewards.

91. ANSWER: D.
PMBOK GUIDE pages 90–92, 8.3.2

> 8.3.2 Tools and Techniques for Quality Control
> .1 Inspection.
> .2 Control charts.
> .3 Pareto diagrams.
> .4 Statistical sampling.
> .5 Flowcharting.
> .6 Trend analysis.

92. ANSWER: A.
PMBOK GUIDE page 83

Project Quality Management includes the processes required to ensure that the project will satisfy the needs for which it was undertaken.

93. ANSWER: C.
PMBOK GUIDE page 83

Quality Assurance—evaluating overall project performance on a regular basis to provide confidence that the project will satisfy the relevant quality standards.

PROJECT HUMAN RESOURCES MANAGEMENT ANSWERS

94. ANSWER: D.

PMBOK GUIDE page 20, 2.4, and
page 23, 2.4.1

- Managing work relationships through motivation, delegation, supervision, team building, conflict management, and other techniques (20).

2.4.1 Leading

Kotter [4] distinguishes between *leading* and *managing* while emphasizing the need for both: one without the other is likely to produce poor results. He says that managing is primarily concerned with "consistently producing key results expected by stakeholders," while leading involves:

- Establishing direction—developing both a vision of the future and strategies for producing the changes needed to achieve that vision.
- Aligning people—communicating the vision by words and deeds to all those whose cooperation may be needed to achieve the vision.
- Motivating and inspiring—helping people energize themselves to overcome political, bureaucratic, and resource barriers to change (23).

95. ANSWER: D.
PMBOK GUIDE page 98, 9.2.1.2

When the project management team is able to influence or direct staff assignments, it must consider the characteristics of the potentially available staff. Considerations include, but are not limited to:

- Previous experience—have the individuals or groups done similar or related work before? Have they done it well?
- Personal interests—are the individuals or groups interested in working on this project?
- Personal characteristics—are the individuals or groups likely to work well together as a team?
- Availability—will the most desirable individuals or groups be available in the necessary time frames?

96. ANSWER: B.
PMBOK GUIDE page 94, paragraph 2,
and page 96, 9.1.2

- Human resource administrative activities are seldom a direct responsibility of the project management team (94).

Many organizations have a variety of policies, guidelines, and procedures that can help the project management team with various aspects of organizational planning. For example, an organization that views managers as "coaches" is likely to have documentation on how the role of "coach" is to be performed (96).

97. ANSWER: C.
PMBOK GUIDE page 18, figure 2-6,
and page 20

Weak matrices maintain many of the characteristics of a functional organization and the project manager role is more that of a coordinator or expediter than that of a manager. In similar fashion, strong matrices have many of the characteristics of the projectized organization—full-time project managers with considerable authority and full-time project administrative staff.

98. ANSWER: D.
PMBOK GUIDE page 97, 9.1.3.2

Particular attention should be paid to how project team members (individuals or groups) will be released when they are no longer needed on the project. Appropriate reassignment procedures may:
- Reduce costs by reducing or eliminating the tendency to "make work" to fill the time between this assignment and the next.
- Improve morale by reducing or eliminating uncertainty about future employment opportunities.

99. ANSWER: D.
PMBOK GUIDE page 100, 9.3.2.3

Projects must often have their own reward and recognition systems since the systems of the performing organization may not be appropriate. For example, the willingness to work overtime in order to meet an aggressive schedule objective *should* be rewarded or recognized; needing to work overtime as the result of poor planning *should not* be.

100. ANSWER: A.

PMBOK GUIDE page 4; page 11;
page 15, 2.2; and page 18, 2.3.3

Projects are often critical components of the performing organization's business strategy (4).

Projects and project management operate in an environment broader than that of the project itself. The project management team must understand this broader context. . . . (11)

The project management team must identify the stakeholders, determine what their needs and expectations are, and then manage and influence those expectations to ensure a successful project. . . . Key stakeholders on every project include:

- Performing organization—the enterprise whose employees are most directly involved in doing the work of the project.
- Sponsor—the individual or group within the performing organization who provides the financial resources, in cash or in kind, for the project (15).

The structure of the performing organization often constrains the availability of or terms under which resources become available to the project (18).

101. ANSWER: E.

PMBOK GUIDE page 100, 9.3.2.4

Collocation involves placing all, or almost all, of the most active project team members in the same physical location to enhance their ability to perform as a team. Collocation is widely used on larger projects and can also be effective for smaller projects (e.g., with a "war room" where the team congregates or leaves in-process work items).

102. ANSWER: A.

PMBOK GUIDE page 20, 2.3.3, and page 95, 9.1.1.3

In similar fashion, strong matrices have many of the characteristics of the projectized organization—full-time project managers with considerable authority and full-time project administrative staff (20).

• Organizational structure of the performing organization—an organization whose basic structure is a *strong matrix* means a relatively stronger role for the project manager than one whose basic structure is a *weak matrix*. . . . (95)

103. ANSWER: E.
PMBOK GUIDE page 93, paragraph 1

Project Human Resource Management includes the processes required to make the mos effective use of the people involved with the project. . . . the following major processes:
9.1 Organizational Planning—identifying, documenting, and assigning project roles, responsibilities, and reporting relationships.
9.2 Staff Acquisition—getting the human resources needed assigned to and working on the project.
9.3 Team Development—developing individual and group skills to enhance project performance.

104. ANSWER: D.
PMBOK GUIDE pages 98–99, 9.2.1,
9.2.2, and 9.2.3

9.2.1 Inputs to Staff Acquisition
.1 Staffing management plan.
.2 Staffing pool description.
.3 Recruitment practices.

9.2.2 Tools and Techniques for Staff Acquisition
.1 Negotiations.
.2 Pre-assignment.
.3 Procurement.

9.2.3 Outputs from Staff Acquisition
.1 Project staff assigned.
.2 Project team directory.

105. ANSWER: E.
PMBOK GUIDE pages 96–98, 9.1.2
and 9.1.3

9.1.2 Tools and Techniques for Organizational Planning
.1 Templates. Although each project is unique, most projects will resemble another project to some extent. Using the role and responsibility definitions or reporting relationships of a similar project can help expedite the process of organizational planning.

9.1.3 Outputs from Organizational Planning
.1 Role and responsibility assignments.
.2 Staffing management plan.
.3 Organization chart.
.4 Supporting detail.

106. ANSWER: C.
PMBOK GUIDE page 99, 9.3

Team development on a project is often complicated when individual team members are accountable to both a functional manager and to the project manager. . . . Effective management of this dual reporting relationship is often a critical success factor for the project and is generally the responsibility of the project manager.

107. ANSWER: D.
PMBOK GUIDE page 18, 2.3.2; page 20, 2.3.3; page 95, 9.1.1.3; and page 96, 9.1.3

A project manager with a highly participative style is apt to encounter problems in a rigidly hierarchical organization, while a project manager with an authoritarian style will be equally challenged in a participative organization (18).

In a projectized organization, team members are often collocated. Most of the organization's resources are involved in project work, and project managers have a great deal of independence and authority (20).

Common factors that may constrain how the team is organized include, but are not limited to, the following:
• Organizational structure of the performing organization—an organization whose basic structure is a *strong matrix* means a relatively stronger role for the project manager than one whose basic structure is a *weak matrix*. . . . (95)

The roles and responsibilities of the project manager are generally critical on most projects but vary significantly by application area (96).

108. ANSWER: C.
PMBOK GUIDE page 18, Figure 2-6; page 19, Figure 2-8; and page 20, 2.3.3

At the opposite end of the spectrum is the *projectized organization* shown in **Figure 2-8**. In a projectized organization, team members are often collocated. Most of the organization's resources are involved in project work, and project managers have a great deal of independence and authority (20).

109. ANSWER: D.
PMBOK GUIDE page 19, Figure 2.7; Glossary, pages 164 and 165

Functional Manager. A manager responsible for activities in a specialized department or function (e.g., engineering, manufacturing, marketing).

Matrix Organization. Any organizational structure in which the project manager shares responsibility with the functional managers for assigning priorities and for directing the work of individuals assigned to the project.

PROJECT COMMUNICATIONS MANAGEMENT ANSWERS

110. ANSWER: B.
PMBOK GUIDE page 103, paragraph 1,
page 104, Figure 10-1

Figure 10-1 provides an overview of the following major processes:

10.1 Communications Planning—determining the information and communications needs of the stakeholders; who needs what information, when will they need it, and how will it be given to them.

10.2 Information Distribution—making needed information available to project stakeholders in a timely manner.

10.3 Performance Reporting—collecting and disseminating performance information. This includes status reporting, progress measurement, and forecasting.

10.4 Administrative Closure—generating, gathering, and disseminating information to formalize phase or project completion.

11. ANSWER: C.
PMBOK GUIDE page 105, 10.1.1.2, and
page 107, 10.2.2.3

The technologies or methods used to transfer
information back and forth among project
elements can vary significantly: from brief
conversations to extended meetings, from
simple written documents to immediately
accessible on-line schedules and databases
(105).

Information can be shared by team members
through a variety of methods including manual
filing systems, electronic text databases, project
management software, and systems which
allow access to technical documentation such
as engineering drawings (107).

Project information may be distributed using a
variety of methods including project meetings,
hard copy document distribution, shared
access to networked electronic databases, fax,
electronic mail, voice mail, and video
conferencing (107).

112. ANSWER: A.

Adams, John R., and Nicki S. Kirchof. 1997. Conflict Management for Project Managers. In *Principles of Project Management*. Upper Darby, PA.: Project Management Institute. (pages 181–183)

The antecedent conditions of conflict were previously defined in general terms. They are particularly apparent in the project and matrix organizations. Ambiguous jurisdictions, for example, are especially prevalent in the matrix organization. In this structure, the limits of each party's jurisdictions are purposely ambiguous since each person is responsible to different people for different things (181).

Communication barriers are the most often discussed condition leading to conflict in matrix and project structures. These barriers exist to a great degree if the parties are separated from each other, either physically or by the timing of their contributions to the project. In a project environment, functional and project managers frequently physically perform their work many miles apart, with the project manager typically located at the project site and the functional manager at the corporate offices. Further, people with different skills are required to contribute to the project at different times (182).

When two parties must make a joint decision, the possibility of conflict is increased. In a project environment, joint decisions concerning the allocation and sharing of project personnel must be made jointly by the project and functional managers. Similar joint decisions must be made among top management, the project manager, and functional managers relative to all resources. This situation increases the need for close, face-to-face contact among the managers and can thus lead to increased conflict (183).

113. ANSWER: D.
PMBOK GUIDE page 106, 10.1.3.1

A communications management plan is a document which provides:

- A collection and filing structure which details what methods will be used to gather and store various types of information. Procedures should also cover collecting and disseminating updates and corrections to previously distributed material.
- A distribution structure which details to whom information (status reports, data, schedule, technical documentation, etc.) will be used to distribute various types of information. This structure must be compatible with the responsibilities and reporting relationships described by the project organization chart.
- A description of the information to be distributed, including format, content, level of detail, and conventions/definitions to be used.
- Production schedules showing when each type of communication will be produced.
- Methods for accessing information between scheduled communications.
- A method for updating and refining the communications management plan as the project progresses and develops.

114. ANSWER: C.

Kimmons, R. L. 1990. *Project Management Basics, a Step by Step Approach*. New York: Marcel Dekker, Inc. (pages 175–176)

> The project manager has three principal interests in establishing and maintaining good document control and handling on his projects.
> (1) **Effective communication** on the job. . . .
> (2) The ever-increasing need to be able to **reconstruct why certain decisions were made** as they were.
> (3) **Historical value** that the documentation may have in running and organizing future like jobs.

115. ANSWER: D.

Kimmons, R.L. 1990. *Project Management Basics, a Step by Step Approach*. New York: Marcel Dekker, Inc. (page 304)

We can improve our listening ability by doing these things:
- Show the speaker that you are interested by demonstrating active, supportive attention to what he has to say.
- Even though you are busy and have your own problems, listen.
- Don't constantly interrupt the speaker or try to finish his sentences by leaping ahead with your own thoughts, and don't occupy yourself with busywork or fidgeting while you are supposed to be listening.
- Listen for the concepts and the ideas being presented by the speaker. Don't concentrate exclusively on the facts he is using to support his arguments.
- Make sure that there is sufficient feedback on both sides to assure that the points being made are clearly understood.

116. ANSWER: D.

Kimmons, R. L. 1990. *Project Management Basics, a Step by Step Approach.* New York: Marcel Dekker, Inc. (page 301)

Communication involves at least two people who may have very different backgrounds, experience, and education. Many times these individuals come from different cultures, speak different languages, and certainly have different drives.

Unclear Expectations. One of the root problems with communication occurs when that the manager is not clear in his own mind what he wants. Under pressure of time, he has not been able to adequately analyze the requirements and so he prematurely assigns the work. If he does not know what he expects, there is little chance that he will explain it satisfactorily to the employee. The manager is able to sort out his ideas afterward, but frequently does not go back and talk to the employee about them.

117. ANSWER: B.

Stuckenbruck, Linn, C., and David Marshall. 1997. Team Building for Project Managers. In *Principles of Project Management*. Upper Darby, PA.: Project Management Institute (page 152)

Communication blockers. Too many innovative ideas are smothered by negative thinking before they are given any chance to prove their worth. It is much easier to think of dozens of reasons why something will not work than to figure out how to make it work. People who are prone to this type of thinking, particularly if they overdo the "devil's advocate" role, will act as communication blockers and seriously impede the process of team building. These people announce their presence by their typical negative responses when something new is suggested. The following types of responses have been termed "idea killers":

- It's been done before.
- It will never work.
- The boss won't like it.
- That's interesting, but . . .
- It will never fly.
- It will cost a fortune.
- Let's be realistic.

18. ANSWER: B.

Stuckenbruck, Linn C., and David Marshall. 1997. Team Building for Project Managers. In *Principles of Project Management*. Upper Darby, PA.: Project Management Institute (page 136)

It is generally accepted that the project manager is the one person responsible for the project team's guidance, motivation, output, and control. This statement implies that the project manager is all of the following:

- Leader
- Project's technical director
- System integrator
- Project planner
- Project administrator
- Team's communications expediter
- Mender of fractured relationships
- Team's "den mother."

119. ANSWER: A.

Adams, John R., and Nicki S. Kirchof. 1997. Conflict Management for Project Managers. In *Principles of Project Management.* Upper Darby, PA.: Project Management Institute (page 174 and page 192)

> Conflict is generally defined as "a clash between hostile or opposing elements of ideas."[8] As applied to human behavior it is a disagreement between individuals, which can vary from a mild disagreement to a win/lose, emotion-packed confrontation. There are two basic, but opposing, views of conflict, the traditional and the modern (see Figure 3). The traditional view sees conflict as being primarily negative. In this view, conflict is caused by troublemakers; it is bad; and it should be avoided. The manager who views conflict in this way avoids admitting that it exists, keeps it under cover, and tries to suppress it. The contemporary view sees conflict in a more positive light. According to this view, conflict is inevitable. It is a natural result of change and is frequently beneficial to the manager if properly managed. In particular, an atmosphere of tension, and hence conflict, is essential in any organization committed to developing or working with new ideas, for innovation is simply the process of bringing together differing ideas and perspectives into a new and different synthesis (174).
> Withdrawal tends to minimize conflict, but as stated earlier also fails to resolve the issue (192).

20. ANSWER: A.

PMBOK GUIDE page 104, figure 10-1, and page 105–106, 10.1.1

10.1.1 Inputs to Communications Planning

.1 *Communications requirements.*
.2 *Communications technology.*
.3 *Constraints.*
.4 *Assumptions.*

21. ANSWER: D.

PMBOK GUIDE page 23, 2.4.2

Communicating involves the exchange of information.

22. ANSWER: D.

PMBOK GUIDE page 107, 10.2.2.2

Information retrieval systems. Information can be shared by team members through a variety of methods including manual filing systems, electronic text databases, project management software, and systems which allow access to technical documentation such as engineering drawings.

123. ANSWER: E.

Stuckenbruck, Linn C., and David Marshall. 1997, Team Building for Project Managers. In *Principles of Project Management.* Upper Darby, PA.: Project Management Institute (page 151)

> Most project managers spend approximately 90 percent of their working hours engaged in some form of communication: conferences, meetings, writing memos, reading reports, and talking with team members' top management, customers, clients, subcontractors, suppliers, etc.

24. ANSWER: A.

Stuckenbruck, Linn C., and David Marshall. 1997. Team Building for Project Managers. In *Principles of Project Management*. Upper Darby, PA.: Project Management Institute (page 151)

Of course, project managers must be good communicators. This does not mean that they must be orators or spellbinders, but it does mean three things:

- They must recognize the importance of the interpersonal communication network with the project team, and encourage, not inhibit, informal communication between team members.
- They must recognize the importance of human relations to the success of communication flow and team building. Effective communication will not be achieved if there is not harmony and trust.
- They must recognize that communication is a two-way street. The project manager does not just give orders; the project team must understand, participate, and agree before teamwork is achieved. Feedback in both directions is necessary for team building and is vital for a continuing team effort.

125. ANSWER: A.

Stuckenbruck, Linn C., and David Marshall. 1997. Team Building for Project Managers. In *Principles of Project Management*. Upper Darby, PA.: Project Management Institute (page 152)

The term "tight matrix" refers to a matrix where all of the team members are brought together in one location.

126. ANSWER: A.

Cable, Dwayne P., and John R. Adams. 1997. Organizing for Project Management. In *Principles of Project Management*. Upper Darby, PA.: Project Management Institute (page 14)

The project expeditor's primary responsibility lies in the area of communications.

127. ANSWER: C.

PMBOK GUIDE page 105, 10.1.1.2

Communications technology factors which may affect the project include:
- The immediacy of the need for information. . .
- The availability of technology. . . . .
- The expected project staffing. . . .
- The length of the project. . . .

28. ANSWER: C.

dams, John R., and Nicki S. Kirchof. 1997. Conflict
Management for Project Managers. In Principles of
roject Management. Upper Darby, PA.: Project
Management Institute (page 179)

> *Problem solving* (or confrontation) is a mode
> where the disagreement is addressed directly
> . . . . This method is considered theoretically
> to be the best way of dealing with conflict
> because both parties can be fully satisfied if
> they can work together to find a solution that
> meets both of their needs.

29. ANSWER: B.

PMBOK GUIDE page 108, 10.3.2

10.3.2 Tools and Techniques for Performance Reporting

.1 *Performance reviews.*

.2 *Variance analysis.*

.3 *Trend analysis.*

.4 *Earned value analysis.*

.5 *Information distribution tools and
   techniques.*

130. ANSWER: C.
PMBOK GUIDE page 107, 10.2.2.1

The sender is responsible for making the information clear, unambiguous, and complete so that the receiver can receive it correctly and for confirming that it is properly understood.

131. ANSWER: D.
PMBOK GUIDE page 105, 10.1.1.1

Information typically required to determine project communications requirements includes:
- Project organization and stakeholder responsibility relationships.
- Disciplines, departments, and specialties involved in the project.
- Logistics of how many individuals will be involved with the project and at which locations.
- External information needs (e.g., communicating with the media).

32. ANSWER: A.

MBOK GUIDE page 109, 10.4

Administrative closure consists of verifying and documenting project results to formalize acceptance of the product of the project by the sponsor, client, or customer.

PROJECT RISK MANAGEMENT ANSWERS

133. ANSWER: E.
PMBOK GUIDE page 119, 11.3

Risk response development involves defining enhancement steps for opportunities and responses to threats. Responses to threats generally fall into one of three categories:
- Avoidance. . . .
- Mitigation. . . .
- Acceptance. . . .

134. ANSWER: A.
PMBOK GUIDE page 119, 11.3

- Mitigation—reducing the expected monetary value of a risk event by reducing the probability of occurrence (e.g., using proven technology to lessen the probability that the product of the project will not work), reducing the risk event value (e.g., buying insurance), or both.

135. ANSWER: B.
PMBOK GUIDE page 111, 11.1

Risk identification is not a one-time event; it should be performed on a regular basis throughout the project.

136. ANSWER: E.
PMBOK GUIDE page 115, 11.2.2.1

Expected monetary value, as a tool for risk quantification, is the product of two numbers:
- Risk event probability—an estimate of the probability that a given risk event will occur.
- Risk event value. . . .

137. ANSWER: D.

PMBOK GUIDE page 111

Project Risk Management includes the processes concerned with identifying, analyzing, and responding to project risk. It includes maximizing the results of positive events and minimizing the consequences of adverse events. **Figure 11–1** provides an overview of the following major processes:

11.1 Risk Identification. . . .

11.2 Risk Quantification. . . .

11.3 Risk Response Development. . . .

11.4 Risk Response Control. . . .

138. ANSWER: A.
PMBOK GUIDE pages 120–121, 11.3.3

11.3.3 Outputs from Risk Response Development

.1 *Risk management plan.*

.2 *Inputs to other processes.*

.3 *Contingency plans.*

.4 *Reserves.* A reserve is a provision in the project plan to mitigate cost and/or schedule risk. The term is often used with a modifier (e.g., management reserve, contingency reserve, schedule reserve) to provide further detail on what types of risk are meant to be mitigated. . . .

.5 *Contractual agreements.* Contractual agreements may be entered into for insurance, services, and other items as appropriate in order to avoid or mitigate threats. Contractual terms and conditions will have a significant effect on the degree of risk reduction.

139. ANSWER: E.
PMBOK GUIDE page 112, Figure 11.1, and pages
115–117, 11.2.2

> **11.2.2 Tools and Techniques for Risk
> Quantification**
> .1 *Expected monetary value.*
> .2 *Statistical sums.*
> .3 *Simulation.*
> .4 *Decision trees.*
> .5 *Expert judgment.*

140. ANSWER: B.
PMBOK GUIDE page 111

> Risk response development is sometimes called
> response planning or risk mitigation.

141. ANSWER: C.
PMBOK GUIDE page 115, 11.2.1.1

> Stakeholder risk tolerances provide a screen
> for both inputs and outputs to risk
> quantification.

142. ANSWER: A.
PMBOK GUIDE page 117, 11.2.3.1

11.2.3 Outputs from Risk Quantification

.1 *Opportunities to pursue, threats to respond to.* The major output from risk quantification is a list of opportunities that should be pursued and threats that require attention.

.2 *Opportunities to ignore, threats to accept.* The risk quantification process should also document (a) those sources of risk and risk events that the project management team has consciously decided to accept or ignore and (b) who made the decision to do so.

143. ANSWER: D.
PMBOK GUIDE page 119, 11.3

Acceptance—accepting the consequences. Acceptance can be active (e.g., by developing a contingency plan to execute should the risk event occur) or passive (e.g., by accepting a lower profit if some activities overrun).

144. ANSWER: A.
PMBOK GUIDE page 114, 11.1.3

11.1.3 Outputs from Risk Identification
.1 *Sources of risk.*
.2 *Potential risk events.*
.3 *Risk symptoms.*
.4 *Inputs to other processes.*

145. ANSWER: A.
PMBOK GUIDE page 113, 11.1.1.1

The nature of the product of the project will
have a major effect on the risks identified.
Products that involve proven technology will,
all other things being equal, involve less risk
than products which require innovation or
invention.

146. ANSWER: A.
PMBOK GUIDE page 113, 11.1.1.3

Historical information about what actually
happened on previous projects can be
especially helpful in identifying potential risks.

147. ANSWER: C.
PMBOK GUIDE page 113, 11.1.1.2

The outputs of the processes in other
knowledge areas should be reviewed to
identify possible risks. For example:
- Work breakdown structure. . . .
- Cost estimates and duration estimates. . . .
- Staffing plan. . . .
- Procurement management plan. . . .

148. ANSWER: D.
PMBOK GUIDE page 114, 11.1.3.2

Descriptions of potential risk events should
generally include estimates of (a) the
probability that the risk event will occur, (b)
the alternative possible outcomes, (c) expected
timing of the event, and (d) anticipated
frequency (i.e., can it happen more than once).

149. ANSWER: A.
PMBOK GUIDE page 115, 11.2.2.1

Expected monetary value, as a tool for risk quantification, is the product of two numbers:
- Risk event probability—an estimate of the probability that a given risk event will occur.
- Risk event value—an estimate of the gain or loss that will be incurred if the risk event does occur.

150. ANSWER: D.
PMBOK GUIDE page 120, 11.3.2

11.3.2 Tools and Techniques for Risk Response Development
.1 *Procurement.* Procurement, acquiring goods or services from outside the immediate project organization, is often an appropriate response to some types of risk. For example, risks associated with using a particular technology may be mitigated by contracting with an organization that has experience with that technology.
.2 *Contingency planning.* . . .
.3 *Alternative strategies.* . . .
.4 *Insurance.* . . .

151. ANSWER: B.
PMBOK GUIDE page 120, 11.3.3.1

The risk management plan should document
the procedures that will be used to manage risk
throughout the project. In addition to documenting the results of the risk identification
and risk quantification processes, it should
cover who is responsible for managing various
areas of risk, how the initial identification and
quantification outputs will be maintained, how
contingency plans will be implemented, and
how reserves will be allocated.

152. ANSWER: A.
PMBOK GUIDE page 120, 11.3.3.1

A risk management plan may be formal or
informal, highly detailed or broadly framed,
based on the needs of the project. It is a
subsidiary element of the overall project plan. . .

PROJECT PROCUREMENT MANAGEMENT ANSWERS

153. ANSWER: D.
PMBOK GUIDE pages 125–126, 12.1.1

12.1.1 Inputs to Procurement Planning
.1 *Scope statement.* . . .
.2 *Product description.* . . .
.3 *Procurement resources.* . . .
.4 *Market conditions.* . . .
.5 *Other planning outputs.* To the extent that other planning outputs are available, they must be considered during procurement planning. Other planning outputs which must often be considered include preliminary cost and schedule estimates, quality management plans, cash flow projections, the work breakdown structure, identified risks, and planned staffing.
.6 *Constraints.* Constraints are factors that limit the buyer's options. One of the most common constraints for many projects is funds availability.
.7 *Assumptions.*

154. ANSWER: D.
PMBOK GUIDE page 128, 12.2.3.1

Procurement documents should be structured to facilitate accurate and complete responses from prospective sellers. They should always include the relevant statement of work, a description of the desired form of the response, and any required contractual provisions (e.g., a copy of a model contract, non-disclosure provisions).

155. ANSWER: C.
PMBOK GUIDE page 128, 12.2.3.1

The terms "bid" and "quotation" are generally used when the source selection decision will be price-driven (as when buying commercial items), while the term "proposal" is generally used when non-financial considerations such as technical skills or approach are paramount (as when buying professional services).

156. ANSWER: D.
PMBOK GUIDE page 132, 12.5.1.3

Change requests may include modifications to the terms of the contract or to the description of the product or service to be provided. If the seller's work is unsatisfactory, a decision to terminate the contract would also be handled as a change request.

157. ANSWER: C.
PMBOK GUIDE page 129, 12.3.2.2

Existing lists of potential sellers can often be expanded by placing advertisements in general circulation publications such as newspapers or in specialty publications such as professional journals. Some government jurisdictions require public advertising of certain types of procurement items; most government jurisdictions require public advertising of subcontracts on a government contract.

158. ANSWER: A.

Cavendish, Penny , and Martin D. Martin. 1997. Negotiating & Contracting for Project Management. In *Principles of Project Management.* Upper Darby, PA.: Project Management Institute (page 230)

Generally speaking, buyers prefer the fixed price contract, which places more risk on the seller, and sellers prefer cost contracts, which place more risk on the buyer.

The cost-plus-percentage-of-cost contract provides for reimbursement to the contractor for allowable costs due to contract performance. Additionally, the contractor receives an agreed-upon percentage of the estimated cost as profit. From the buyer's standpoint, this is the most undesirable type of contract because the seller has no incentive to decrease costs.

159. ANSWER: C.

Cavendish, Penny, and Martin D. Martin. 1997.
Negotiating & Contracting for Project Management. In
Principles of Project Management. Upper Darby, PA.:
Project Management Institute (page 239)

Fait accompli may be a tactic. One party may
claim that what is being asked for has already
been accomplished and cannot be changed.
For example, a supplier may say he or she
shipped the order because he or she knew that
was what the buyer wanted, therefore it is not
a necessary issue to be negotiated.

160. ANSWER: B.

Martin, Martin D., C. Claude Teagarden, and Charles F. Lambreth. 1997. Contract Administration For The Project Manager. In *Principles of Project Management*. Upper Darby, PA.: Project Management Institute (page 272)

The concept of warranty is based upon one party's assurance to the other that the goods will meet certain standards of quality; including condition, reliability, description, function, or performance.

This assurance may be express or implied. Recognizing the principal function of a warranty is to establish a level of quality (and title—not discussed herein); it thus gives a source of remedy for loss due to a defect in the quality of the goods. The contract may and should establish a level of quality, and if it does, it is an express warranty recognized under Section 2–313 (1) (a) of the Uniform Commercial Code.

161. ANSWER: D.
PMBOK GUIDE page 132, 12.5.2.3

Payments to the seller are usually handled by
the accounts payable system of the performing
organization. On larger projects with many or
complex procurement requirements, the project may develop its own system. In either case,
the system must include appropriate reviews
and approvals by the project management team.

162. ANSWER: C.
PMBOK GUIDE page 133, 12.6.3.2

The person or organization responsible for
contract administration should provide the
seller with formal written notice that the
contract has been completed. Requirements for
formal acceptance and closure are usually
defined in the contract.

163. ANSWER: B.
PMBOK GUIDE page 126, 12.1.2.3

Fixed price or lump sun contracts—this category of contract involves a fixed total price for a well-defined product. To the extent that the product is not well-defined, both the buyer and seller are at risk—the buyer may not receive the desired product or the seller may need to incur additional costs in order to provide it. Fixed price contracts may also include incentives for meeting or exceeding selected project objectives such as schedule targets.

164. ANSWER: C.
PMBOK GUIDE page 133, 12.6.1.1

12.6.1 Inputs to Contract Close-out
.1 *Contract documentation.* Contract documentation includes, but is not limited to, the contract itself along with all supporting schedules, requested and approved contract changes, any seller-developed technical documentation, seller performance reports, financial documents such as invoices and payment records, and the results of any contract-related inspections.

165. ANSWER: C.
PMBOK GUIDE page 133, 12.5.3.2

Changes (approved and unapproved) are fed back through the appropriate project planning and project procurement processes, and the project plan or other relevant documentation is updated as appropriate.

166. ANSWER: A.

PMBOK GUIDE page 133, 12.6.2.1

12.6.2 Tools and Techniques for Contract Close-out

.1 *Procurement audits.* A procurement audit is a structured review of the procurement process from procurement planning through contract administration. The objective of a procurement audit is to identify successes and failures that warrant transfer to other procurement items on this project or to other projects within the performing organization.

167. ANSWER: E.

PMBOK GUIDE pages 128–129, 12.2.3.2

Evaluation criteria may be limited to purchase price if the procurement item is known to be readily available from a number of acceptable sources. . . . When this is not the case, other criteria must be identified and documented to support an integrated assessment. For example:

- Understanding of need. . . .
- Overall or life cycle cost. . . .
- Technical capability. . . .
- Management approach. . . .
- Financial capacity. . . .

168. ANSWER: D.

PMBOK GUIDE pages 130–131, 12.4.2

12.4.2 Tools and Techniques for Source Selection

.1 *Contract negotiation.* Contract negotiation involves clarification and mutual agreement on the structure and requirements of the contract prior to the signing of the contract. To the extent possible, final contract language should reflect all agreements reached. Subjects covered generally include, but are not limited to, responsibilities and authorities, applicable terms and law, technical and business management approaches, contract financing, and price. For complex procurement items, contract negotiation may be an independent process with inputs (e.g., an issues or open items list) and outputs (e.g., memorandum of understanding) of its own. Contract negotiation is a special case of the general management skill called "negotiation. . . . "

.2 *Weighting system.* . . .

.3 *Screening system.* . . .

.4 *Independent estimates.* . . .

169. ANSWER: D.
PMBOK GUIDE page 132, 12.5.1.3

Contested changes, those where the seller and
the project management team cannot agree on
compensation for the change, are variously
called claims, disputes, or appeals.

170. ANSWER: C.
PMBOK GUIDE Glossary, page 158

FFP Firm Fixed Price